Different Daughters

A Book by Mothers of Lesbians

Edited by Louise Rafkin

Cleis Press
Pittsburgh • San Francisco

Published in the United States by Cleis Press, P.O. Box 8933, Pittsburgh, Pennsylvania 15221, and P.O. Box 14684, San Francisco, California 94114.

First Edition.
10 9 8 7 6 5 4 3 2 1

"Purple Balloons on Market Street," by Constance Shepard Jolly, originally appeared in *Wellesley Magazine*, the alumnae publication of Wellesley College, Summer 1984.

© Poem by Sappho, translated by Mary Barnard. University of California Press. Used by permission.

Cover art and text illustrations: Pacha Wasiolek
Cover and text design: Louise Rafkin (with Frédérique Delacoste)
Back cover photos: Jan Probst

Printed in the United States.

ISBN: 0-939416-12-3 21.95 cloth
ISBN: 0-939416-13-1 8.95 paper
Library of Congress Catalog Card Number: 86-72846

This book is available on tape to disabled women from the Womyn's Braille Press, P.O. Box 8475, Minneapolis, Minnesota 55408.

Different Daughters

Acknowledgments:

I would like to thank Pacha Wasiolek for her love and unfailing encouragement for all my creative endeavors. In addition, her patience with me and my (many!) willful ideas during the production of the powerful cover art was more than commendable. Appreciation and kudos to color separator Kris Kovich whose skill and generosity allowed us to present such a beautiful book.

I am grateful to Jan Probst, Rachel Lurie, Lila Struss and Bridget Boylan for their help proofreading. Many thanks to Jennifer Krebs who, in addition to editing and proofreading, served as on-call reference librarian while working her post at Old Wives' Tales women's bookstore. Sunday Von Drasek's typesetting skills and stamina were also very much appreciated.

Working with the women of Cleis has been great. My thanks to Felice Newman and especially to Frédérique Delacoste whose cooperation and humor in the face of my designer's neurosis was extremely admirable.

It is due to the courage and love of the women who contributed to this book that my project was realized. My heartfelt gratitude goes out to them for sharing their lives.

For Rhoda,
and Ruth

Sleep, darling

I have a small
daughter called

Cleis, who is
like a golden
flower
        I wouldn't
take all Croesus'
kingdom with love
thrown in, for her

        — Sappho

Contents

Notes From A Different Daughter

by Louise Rafkin

T his book had twin beginnings.

One drizzly day nearly five years ago, I sat in the kitchen of my six-lesbian household in Auckland, New Zealand, musing with my roommates about our mothers' lack of understanding of our lives. Our mothers expressed different levels of acceptance, ranging from those who knew about our homosexuality and visited with us, to others who knew nothing about our lifestyle and rarely set foot in the door. My own mother lived far away and wrote politely accepting letters. There was one mother who had not yet been told, and continued in seemingly blissful ignorance despite obvious clues. Before her visits we raced around "de-dyke-ing" the house, ridding it of lesbian posters, books and other "evidence," rousing couples and warning of slips in conversation.

Meanwhile, in a small-town library in Southern California, my mother was rummaging through bookshelves desperately trying to locate some printed material that would illuminate her understanding of homosexuality and lesbianism, and quell her anger, fear and confusion. The same library that had once happily afforded me feasts of Nancy Drew mysteries and Anatole the Mouse adventures produced nothing more than a handful of dusty volumes, none of which offered her support or understanding. Academic, psychological tomes, they spouted convoluted theories of homosexuality, eager to blame parents searching for ways to explain the nightmare.

Nothing she found supported my claims of a healthy lifestyle and community, full of many wonderful, well-adjusted and strong women — or my own gut-knowledge that nothing was wrong with me.

In my newly come-out lesbian zeal I imagined a book for

mothers that would somehow make everything okay. I wanted my mother to have a how-to book full of easy answers to difficult questions and missives from accepting and fully understanding mothers.

I have learned much in five years.

Though always an optimist, my feet touched ground a couple of years after the kitchen table scene, coincidentally, in the country of my origin. Back in close proximity to my mother, I wished again for something to give her. Despite spending holidays and camping trips with me — and even a few weeks stay in the six-lesbian household — she still had strong feelings of anger and resentment about my lesbianism, as well as lingering confusions and stereotypes. We were both frustrated, but I knew from the experiences of friends and lovers how lucky I was to have a mother who was so accepting and so open to learning.

I sent out a batch of three hundred flyers three years ago, to parents' groups, women's magazines and organizations across the United States and Europe describing the book I wanted to edit and seeking submissions. I stressed that all responses were welcome — from recounts of factual experiences to poetry, prose and fiction. I decided the book was to be written by mothers because I feel mother/daughter relationships are particularly intense and important, different from those between fathers and daughters. Mothers are often the first to know about their daughters' lesbianism, and may in turn become buffers between daughters and other family members.

I waited as the first deadline passed and one submission came on its solo flight into my mailbox. Letters of support from daughters came from hither and thither, but the lack of response from mothers bewildered me.

It has taken me nearly to the completion of the book to understand the difficulties in my undertaking.

Having been lucky enough to come out as a lesbian in an era when society is aware and somewhat accepting of homosexuals, and having been fortunate — or strategic — enough to set myself in the midst of San Francisco's lesbian community, I had forgotten the extent to which homosexuality is shamed in this society.

Though the struggle for gay pride has gained momentum and visibility over the last fifteen years, the basis for many mothers' opinions and reactions to lesbianism was formed well before the sixties and seventies. And despite movement toward gay pride and gay rights, current laws and the rise in both fundamentalism and AIDS hysteria assures us that homophobia continues to thrive in the eighties. In June 1986, the Supreme Court upheld the legality of Georgia's anti- sodomy law, maintaining states' rights to legislate morality, especially as it pertains to sexual preference. In essence, the sodomy laws of twenty-five states and the District of Columbia make acknowledged homosexuals admitted felons. Since the recent ruling, the National Gay and Lesbian Task Force has reported an increase in sodomy arrests. The laws, primarily on the books in midwestern and southern states, have rarely been put to the test in lesbian cases, yet presumably they apply to behavior of both lesbians and gay men, as well as heterosexuals whose behavior deviates from the "norm."

The sodomy laws make it difficult to legislate for civil rights in these states, because the state governments do not see a need to sanction rights for felons! The current ruling also allows the

United States military to continue using their own sodomy laws to exclude gays and lesbians, and in many states these laws prohibit openly gay people from receiving certain professional licenses. Of course these laws are also used against gays and lesbians in child custody battles.

The stigma for parents of lesbians carries on persistently as well. Fear of reactions from relatives and friends keeps many mothers hidden in closets. As a testament to that fear, over half the women who ventured out of those closets to be included in this book have opted to use pseudonyms.

I've come to respect the enormity of this project through exposure to the backgrounds and experiences of the women who have contributed. I have met and talked with many wonderful women in the making of this book, and feel as though I have made new friends all across the country. Through breaking out of the safety and sameness of our individual lives, I believe we can come to understand each other. Each chapter is precious to me; each conquered a variety of obstacles, made its way around a black hole of silence and oppression, and found its way into print for other mothers — and daughters — to draw strength from.

In the end the contributors came through personal contacts, friends' mothers, friends of friends, and contact with the Federation of Parents and Friends of Lesbians and Gays (PFLAG). The women in this book range in age from mid-forties to late seventies, and hail from all over the United States, plus New Zealand. A range of racial, class, and religious backgrounds are represented. Many of the pieces are transcribed from interviews. These are marked [*] to set them apart from the written pieces.

The hardest submission for me to edit was — of course — my own mother's. I had done an interview with her early in the project, but continually asked her to re-write her piece, to insert this or that experience which I recounted to her, or this or that attitude I thought had slipped her memory. This made me realize that as a daughter my view of the book is naturally different from that of a mother of a lesbian. For years I referred to the book as the "mothers book," and a title only emerged for the work after I realized that the book was by mothers but about daughters. *Different Daughters* leapt into my heart when I let go of my book about mothers and let the voices of the mothers come through unfiltered by my daughterly vision. I also let go of the urge to shape my mother's piece — which I love. I think she deserves an award, however, for having to endure a most probing editor.

I hope this book offers both support for mothers and understanding for daughters. I am proud to offer these stories, each born of its own hope for the day when loving — despite our differences — is not so unusual as to warrant a book. In many ways these stories are quite ordinary, made extraordinary through their telling.

Louise Rafkin
Oakland, California
January 1987

From Hermit Crabs to Hamsters

by Hazel Brickman

I am seventy-four, married, and live with my husband. I have two children, a daughter, forty-three, and a son, thirty-six, and three teenage grandchildren. I was a high school speech teacher for about forty years, and for the most part loved it. In my retirement I have been involved in Elderhostel Programs (continuing education), yoga, tutoring at the Fortune Society for ex-convicts, traveling, playing tennis, and swimming and sunning in California. Also, I love to eat!

Dear Louise,
  This account of my recollections of the history of the relationship with my lesbian daughter will be in the form of a letter to you. I feel I'll be speaking to a most accepting listener.

First, the facts of the situation. After eleven years of marriage and three children, my daughter fell in love with a mother of three children, married fourteen years. Within one month of physically consummating their relationship, my daughter told me about it. Partly she told me because she and her husband were requesting financial assistance, thinking their marriage might be saved through counseling. Secondly — and this I'm proud of — she knew I would continue to love and accept her, although her lover feared anger and rejection. The remaining facts — both women divorced their husbands and set up a joint household, with two mothers, six children from age three to eleven, and varied pets, from hermit crabs to hamsters. Both at that time retained custody of their children, although the husbands were aware of the lesbian relationship and held it over them in one way or another.

That was about twelve years ago. I can remember, vividly, her taking me for a walk on a misty, summer afternoon when I was visiting her in the country. She indicated she felt an explanation was due me and her Dad as to why her marriage seemed to be floundering. She then explained that she had been unhappy for the entire eleven years of her marriage, had never felt she could tell me, and in the past two years had found a warm, responsive relationship — with another woman — and named her, someone I had known as a close friend of hers. And then she added, most helpfully, "You know, Mom, I'm exactly the same loving daughter that I was five minutes ago, before you knew of this relationship."

First there was shock, for although she had been the tomboy, athletic-type all her life, she had also been very popular with boys and men and had appeared deeply in love with the husband she married. My second reaction was relief. At last the husband whom we felt had never been a compatible choice, would now, probably, be out of the picture. As for the relationship with the woman, we didn't think it likely to continue. It just seemed too out of character for a daughter of ours to be romantically involved with a woman. How little we knew; how little we understood!

The request from my daughter was to convey this information to her Dad. With my head spinning from this turn of events, I returned home that evening and promptly, as gently as I could, using very much my daughter's approach, told my husband. He was flabbergasted and puzzled; tended to believe his daughter had been seduced; was hopeful that she would terminate her marriage; and quite sure, as I was, that this was a "passing fancy" caused by an unhappy marriage.

During the next few years, while I read furiously everything I could find (and my daughter fed me plenty of printed material), her father became bitterly rejecting of her lover. He couldn't abide her personality, even before he knew of the relationship with our daughter. He was sure she was a seductress — and he vetoed her inclusion in family gatherings at our home. This caused deep anguish to my daughter, myself and her lover, and, I'm sure, to my husband.

Our daughter's brother, seven years younger than she, and in his early twenties when she divorced, was baffled by the events. How had she chosen the wrong husband and had three children by him? So my husband and I told him the truth. He had no problems accepting his sister, and now understood the divorce. She eventually talked fully and frankly with him so that, for the first time, brother and sister felt very close.

One of the most difficult episodes was the upset experienced by my husband and I when she told us she had agreed to "come out" on a television program dealing with the civil rights of lesbian mothers. We feared for her job in the New York City school system; we feared rejection of her by students and fellow workers; we feared the effect on her children in their relationships with their peers.

We watched the half-hour program — on a major network — with trepidation. However, we wound up feeling pride in her contribution to the cause of civil liberties, a cause which we had always championed. Not only did she not lose face in the teaching community, but her administration, wisely, recognized her insights so that she was asked to be a resource person for gay and lesbian students with problems.

There was to be a repeat of the program the following week. This time we called friends and relatives, none of whom, to our knowledge, had been aware of her lesbianism, and urged them to watch. To our amazement, we discovered for ourselves the tremendous relief of being "out of the closet." There were only positive results. We were surrounded by wonderful friends who expressed their support.

One area of difficulty, however, was between my husband and myself. I was able to accept our daughter's choice of a mate, although I disapproved strongly of many of this woman's attitudes and ethics, whereas, for my husband, she was an anathema. He had to reject her as a physical presence, not because of her homosexuality, but because of her personality. Because I knew how deeply our daughter felt this rejection of her choice, I suffered her pain, my husband's and my own. It was an unhappy time. The only resolution for this was to spend time with my daughter and her lover alone, without involving my husband.

There were also concerns about how the children — growing into their teens — would handle their mother's lifestyle. We need not have worried. Now, at fourteen, seventeen and nineteen, they appear to be typical, average teenagers, with their typical problems and pursuits.

On the whole, I have found that because my daughter is "out," I am freed so that I may speak up when I hear a homophobic comment. I can educate where I hear lack of information, and I can support where I sense a need.

My life has been enriched by knowing gay and lesbian individuals. Never have I been so close to my daughter, or so able to be honest with her. I can truly say I'm grateful she has found a healthy expression for her sexuality, now with a warm, loving person. I have to say it has made the whole family relationship a happier one, because we find the present person in my daughter's life so wonderful and she is part of our family circle. Our daughter is living a rich, rewarding life with the same level of energy and capability she has always displayed, but with the solid assurance that she has her parents' admiring support.

I appreciate this opportunity to share these experiences in a steadily-strengthening relationship with my daughter.

A Tradition
of Strength

by Doris Thompson *

*I am a black woman,
fifty-three years old, a
graduate of a women's
college. I am retired
from almost thirty years
of federal service, the
last ten years of which
were spent in equal em-
ployment and civil
rights work. I'm now
working independently
as an organization con-
sultant, conducting
training and manage-
ment consultations
around people prob-
lems. I have worked and
lived in mixed racial and
gender situations all my
life. I feel I have an open
philosophy about look-
ing at various lifestyles,
how people live and
what people want.*

Despite my open mind, my first reaction to Margaret's lesbianism was to think it was another life phase for her. The child of a broken marriage, she had recently moved back from living with her father. Our relationship was improving, but it wasn't all that good. I didn't even know she was thinking about coming out. Thinking her lesbianism a stage was the extent of my openness, and I stayed at that point for quite a while. I think now, two years later, I am really just moving out of that attitude. More than just a lifestyle, I now know lesbianism is the way she wants to live, the way she sees herself, the way she is.

I have always had strong role models in my life, grandmothers and great aunts who I saw working and who were not in traditional women's roles — even in their marriages. One of my grandmothers raised her five children as a single parent. She was widowed and though she re-married — unheard of at the time — she later divorced. She was really the matriarch of the family. I think this all has to something do with Margaret and her lifestyle. I love women, and I respect women who are assertive and powerful.

I didn't feel threatened by her choice, but I really wondered how she knew, how she made the decision. We've talked about women being strong and powerful, but that doesn't mean all strong women are lesbians. Many of the qualities about lesbians that she has discussed with me are ones I have seen in a lot of women, and I haven't necessarily thought these women were lesbians. I have these qualities, yet I am a straight woman. That's the part that is still confusing to me.

I didn't ask Margaret directly why she was a lesbian. Now that I have learned more of the things she feels, I think there are a lot of things in her life experience that could have led her to that decision. In me she has a strong role model and she has a grandmother who has been politically active all her life. Margaret's own politics and deep convictions about social responsibility certainly must have contributed to her choice.

Margaret keeps asking me who I have told about her. I have problems about this. If I tell people, they want explanations. It puts you in such a position. I talked about it as if it were a stage with the first friend I told. I still have problems saying, "My daughter is a lesbian."

Margaret loves children and plans to have some, which I feel really good about. When the time comes that she is going to have a child, adopt a child, or raise a child, I know it will bring up the issue with lots of people. Margaret has not yet told her grandmothers and I wouldn't see that as my role, but I do think *I* could talk to my mother about it, and I know that time will come. I know that I am not ashamed of her. I am very proud of her and who she is. Margaret is my daughter and I love her. That love hasn't changed, and never will.

I have met many of Margaret's friends, other women who I want to know and be around. Visiting with her has been so good, though we all do have such stereotypes! It's almost like the way people think about blacks. I guess I see a lot of similarities in the way we look at lots of people. If you don't experience things with people, you think of them as strange or different and therefore you are afraid of them. We have to learn about the lesbian lifestyle. I have much to learn, but I think basically we are all people. We all feel love and pain. We all experience relationships, and there are only degrees of difference between us. My learning about her life is an evolutionary process.

A
Merry-Go-Round

by Fran Harris

I am a retired New York City school teacher and an activist always fighting for human rights. For the past eleven years I have been involved in the Soviet Jewry Movement. I was arrested for peacefully demonstrating in front of the Soviet Mission in Manhattan. As a volunteer, I have taught evening classes in English as a second language to immigrants from all over the world. I love people, laughter, music and dance. My husband is an observant Jew and I keep kosher and observe the Sabbath because it gives him joy. I am not a religious woman. I am a warm, caring and kind human being.

We sat around the dinner table drinking coffee, reminiscing, enjoying being together for the first time in over a year, my husband, my son and my two daughters. We had about two hours before we would have to drive Laurie to the airport. And then our youngest daughter, Joyce, dropped the bomb:

"I have something to tell you," she said. "It's not easy to tell, but I feel that I have to say it now."

We all began to guess, laughingly at first, but then we saw how serious she looked and how her eyes filled up with tears. It was no longer a joke. To each of our guesses Joyce said, "No, it's not that." Then my husband said jokingly, "You're a lesbian, too." When Joyce said, "That's it," the three of us were speechless, in a state of shock.

We had grown accustomed to the fact that our oldest daughter Laurie came out as lesbian three years before, but this was something else. Laurie was a child of the sixties. She had gone through the whole rebellious scene, sampling drugs, campus unrest, several years at a Hindu ashram, several affairs with young men, and a lengthy affair with an older, married man. We were prepared for almost anything as far as Laurie was concerned, because she had led us to expect the unexpected.

The shock of Joyce's disclosure was much harder to handle than anything we had ever known. My first reaction was pain and hurt. How could she have kept this from us for so long? How could she not have trusted me? How she must have suffered when my husband and I spoke about our feelings regarding Laurie's lesbianism. Then I began to realize. Joyce couldn't have told us about herself after Laurie had come out to us. When she saw how devastated we were about Laurie, she had to be silent. How awful it must have been for her when she was forced to date the sons of my friends.

All of us, including Laurie, found it hard to believe that Joyce — the conservative, religious, quiet girl — could be telling us that for many years she had known her preference for women, and that she only went out with men to please her father and me.

My husband, who is conservative and an Orthodox Jew, handled this situation beautifully and with a great deal of self-control. "Don't cry," he said. "We love you." And then, as if it were rehearsed, both of us said, "You're the same girl we've known and have loved all of your life."

We talked, all five of us, around the table. We cried and we hugged and we kissed. A great deal of love was expressed and I could almost feel the relief that Joyce was experiencing. Whatever her father and I were feeling inwardly we kept well hidden and what she saw was a mother and father who loved her and accepted her sexual orientation. She didn't see the hurt and confusion that both of us were experiencing. We kept that inside ourselves until we went upstairs later that night.

That was a sleepless night during which we tried to find answers and tried to comfort one another. One thing we both agreed on was that we would give Joyce our support. My husband tried to tell me that it would all pass away like chicken pox or a bad cold, but I knew differently!

I thought back to the time when I learned about Laurie's lesbianism. Laurie didn't "come out" exactly; it was when I visited her in Florida, where she was living with a female roommate, that I felt something strange and asked her about her relationship with this young woman. I could barely pronounce the word "lesbian"; it was such a dirty word to my way of thinking.

I was devastated to find out my suspicions were well-founded. I think this revelation hurt me more than her involvement in the drug scene and her last affair with the married man. It was all so alien to me. When I was fifteen, I read Radclyffe Hall's novel, *The Well of Loneliness,* but I didn't quite understand it. Other than that, all I knew was that lesbians were disgusting people, ugly women who wore men's clothes and did things to each other that were too horrible to talk about.

But this was something different. Laurie didn't fit my image of a lesbian as a woman who looked, acted, and dressed like a man. Laurie didn't fit this image at all. She was petite, pretty, bright and charming. Laurie had always attracted boys when she was young, and men when she grew older. What happened? Was it something I had done or hadn't done? How could I keep this horrible revelation from my Orthodox, conservative husband who looked forward to the day when Laurie would finally settle down with a nice Jewish boy and raise a family? Who could I speak to? What could I do? Nobody could be told. I had to keep this a secret and deal with it myself.

A busy person doesn't have too much time to brood over things. I was lucky. A full-time job, organization work and a family occupied most of my time. But the secret weighed heavily on my heart. The worst part was not having anyone to talk to. I had so many unanswered questions and so many fears. I looked for books dealing with the subject in the public library, but found nothing that helped in even a small way.

Eventually Laurie told her sister, Joyce, and so I was able to talk to her about some of my feelings. In retrospect I can well imagine how Joyce must have suffered listening to me talk about Laurie.

Then my son was taken into our confidence and finally we all figured a way to break the news to Dad. My husband was angry. "It's a sickness," he said. "It's a result of all her crazy living." He absolutely refused to accept the fact that Laurie called herself a lesbian.

Two miserable years passed and then something wonderful happened. Laurie wrote asking me to come out to San Francisco and attend a conference of Jewish women, and I was able to go. From the first evening, when we attended a gay Shabbat, to the last evening four days later, I was on a merry-go-round. I attended as many workshops as was possible and even unexpectedly conducted one myself. Throughout the conference there was a great deal of warmth expressed. Many of my questions were answered and most of my fears were dispelled. I met lesbians from all walks of life, some with children, some who had been married for years before becoming lesbian, and some who were about to become mothers.

I came home as high as a kite. I was ready to shout out to all my friends and neighbors that my Laurie was fine! That I was no longer upset about the fact that she would never lead a "normal" life. That I was proud of all the things she was doing. That I liked her friends and that I loved her more than ever. I managed to convince my husband not to worry too much about Laurie, and both her sister and brother listened to my experiences with the gay women at the conference. They were pleased to find me in such a good frame of mind.

Then little by little my joy dissipated. When I told my two closest friends about Laurie both said they would not accept that kind of behavior and that I should forbid her to come into my home. I responded by putting these "friends" out of my life for almost a year. It was only after they apologized profusely did I speak to them again. But our relationships will never be the same. When a third friend gave me similar advice, I decided not to speak truthfully to anyone about Laurie again. I think that I was so hurt and disappointed because I expected them to feel the way I was feeling after the conference. This is one of the hardest things I have had to cope with, responding to acquaintances and neighbors who constantly ask me if my daughters are married yet, or if I have any grandchildren.

There is also the religious aspect. While I seldom go to synagogue, my husband attends services every week. The rabbi, a young intelligent man, usually gives a series of lectures each year and I enjoy attending them with my husband. Imagine our feelings when at the first session this year he spoke about the blight on the New York Jewish community — lesbians and gay men! He said we must not allow them to teach in our schools and that we must keep them out of our synagogues. Both of us sat there sick at heart and couldn't wait to get home where we tried to deal with our feelings.

We love our daughters very much. This helps us deal with the many frustrations and heartaches we feel because their lives deviate from the norm. We worry about their futures. We are fortunate now that both Laurie and Joyce have lovers who are wonderful women. I am well aware of the fact that marriages don't last forever, but I do want our girls to have some stability in their lives. We're proud of them both as human beings. They are involved in worthwhile causes. They are loving, kind and considerate women and we are fortunate to have them. I hope that we will continue to be supportive of each other and that other parents of lesbians and gay men will help us create an environment of understanding so that all of our children can live with dignity and respect. I would like the world to accept my daughters, and others like them, for what they are and see them as I do: intelligent, warm, caring, wonderful women.

Of Prejudice and Acceptance

by Maria Garcia *

I'm Latina, a single parent, with two daughters. I'm fifty-six years old and work as a clerk in a large office building. I am a practicing Catholic and a lector and Eucharistic minister in my church.

My oldest daughter, Carrie, told me she was a lesbian when she was eighteen. At the time I was very upset. It was such a new idea. I had always thought I was liberal, and had always lived around gay people in San Francisco's Mission district. Some of my neighbors were gay and I had always respected their choices.

As I am a practicing Catholic, I went to see my priest and told him I felt very depressed after Carrie told me about her lesbianism. My priest suggested that I go to a Parents and Friends of Lesbians and Gays meeting, and I did. I saw that all parents go through similar feelings when they find out their children are lesbian or gay. I began attending the meetings and have been a member for the last four years. I have found that it is all right to love Carrie, but first it was important to understand her life. I really feel that through this organization, and through verbalizing with other parents and reading literature, my daughter and I have become much closer because of my accepting attitude. I have met many fine lesbians and feel quite comfortable with the situation as it is.

For some time, however, I thought that perhaps Carrie was a lesbian because I had sent her to Catholic school and she hadn't had enough exposure to boys her own age. I'm a single parent and my children only saw their father on the weekends, though we had men friends and she has close relationships with her uncles. I thought that perhaps if she had grown up with a male in the house things would have been different. But I have never met anyone I wanted to be involved with. I also wondered if I had been too strict and if I hadn't been home enough for her. I felt this guilt. I got over it by analyzing these fears and finding that they were unfounded. I now believe people are gay because they are born that way. Almost every gay person I have met through the parents' group has said that they knew at a very early age they were gay. It's not something you wake up with one day and decide, "Oh, today I think I'll be a lesbian!"

My daughter lives near enough to me to be able to come over and visit. If there is someone she is terribly fond of, she'll bring her for dinner. There isn't any animosity between us, and she has a good relationship with her younger sister. I work within the Catholic church to improve relations with the gay community, including work with the nuns and priests. Currently, I am involved in a group that works closely with the Archbishop. It's a slow process and more education is needed.

I told my older sister, Carrie's godmother, about Carrie's lesbianism and she is very accepting. She loves Carrie as she is. I haven't told anyone else in my family, because I feel it is for Carrie to tell them. She respects my privacy and she doesn't go around saying, "My mother's heterosexual and celibate," so why should I go around telling people she is a lesbian? I think that is in poor taste. People should be allowed the privacy of choice, of telling who they want.

There are so many people with anti-gay and anti-lesbian feelings. When the topic comes up, I will say something about gay people if I feel that saying something will make a difference. If I see that it won't change people's feelings, I just let the subject drop. There are gay people in the office where I work. In my department there is a gay man who is liked by all, and people don't say anything bad about him, but will say something about other gays. I talk with him about his gayness, and he knows my daughter. He ran into her at a gay dance and asked her if I knew about her lesbianism, and she told him that I accepted her. He and I now have a closer relationship; we talk and stop over drinks. We've always been friends, but there is a closer affinity with someone who is really understanding and accepting.

I was also told about a woman at work who is gay, so I made a special effort to get to know her. Once she let her defenses down, I found her to be warm and friendly. She was hardworking and helped me in several projects. A different woman at work asked me if I knew that the woman was gay. I told her that I had always found her pleasant to work with and that her sexual preference had never once come up in our working relationship. I hope that made her think.

Being Mexican-American, I am a part of a minority group. Many people have a lot of ill-feeling towards us — that we are lazy, or stupid, or other stereotypes. Although I don't hear much of it here in San Francisco, I understand what prejudice can feel like.

I think the recent Supreme Court decision about homosexuality is wrong. I am a Catholic and would not have an abortion, but that doesn't mean other people have to feel the same way I do. This is America and people should have a choice. The government does not have a right to interfere with one's private life. It disturbs me, but now it's done. Can it be undone? I watch television and listen to radio programs about these issues and I hear people say very strong anti-Semitic, anti-gay, anti-Catholic things that are extremely prejudiced. I find it frightening. It's almost the mentality of the time of Hitler. I grew up listening to this kind of prejudice and propaganda and it disturbs me greatly.

I believe you have to accept your children as they are. The more contact that parents have with the gay community, the better relationship they will have with their children. By isolating themselves from their children they can't move to understanding homosexuality. I think it's most important to read about it, and there is literature all over about it — even in the Catholic bookstores.

And I want information from Carrie that will cement our relationship. A close family is part of my heritage. I came from a family of five and my family means a lot to me. I don't want to do anything to damage my very close and intimate relationship with either of my children. They are very honest and open with me. I give them my opinions and if they don't like them they can tell me. I really love my children. I want to help them live through any miserable periods of their lives, to share in their happiness, to be there for them.

After the Initial Shock

by Rhoda Rafkin

After my husband died I returned to teaching full-time. For many years I taught emotionally disturbed youngsters and brain-damaged college students, but am now a marine biology instructor at a marine institute where we see many thousands of children of all ages, introducing them to the excitement of the ecology and animals of the oceans. I love to travel and go to school. Over the past ten years I've studied a strange array of subjects, from ceramics to Chinese cooking, sailing to sign language. There is never enough time to do all the things I want to do!

A few years ago, I received a letter from my daughter, Louise, who was living in New Zealand, hinting that she was in a relationship with a woman. At that particular time my reaction was shock, since she had been in a relationship with a male New Zealander for about five years and I was very fond of him. After the initial shock I felt that it was something she was "going through," but I also remember thinking, "I don't need another problem, why can't my kids be normal?"

I was born and brought up in a very straight-laced New England town where homosexuality wasn't even discussed in "polite society" and this new revelation was a bit shocking. In the early forties we lived on a Navy base where the military fired a lot of lesbians because their alleged "loose morals" marked them as security risks. I had very negative impressions about lesbians, and all I could think of was that they were perverts, more or less. From reading psychology books I also thought they were women who had bad relationships with their fathers, or men in general, and Louise had some very pleasant experiences with men and got on well with her father. I just didn't know what else to think. One of my dearest friends lives in New Zealand and she wrote and said what wonderful friends my daughter had, and that I needn't worry about her. That was very important to me.

I knew Louise was very committed to the women's movement, and I thought maybe this relationship with a woman was one of her strong statements, since she never does things half-way. I certainly hoped it was merely a "statement," and she did state in her letters that some of her actions were political. I went to check out some information on the subject of lesbianism and couldn't find one good book in our local conservative small town library. All the while in the back of my mind

I kept thinking it would go away with time. Louise was so far away, and I didn't have to face the reality of the situation.

Being widowed for several years, I felt the need for someone to confide in. I am really fortunate in having two wonderfully kind and compassionate women friends with whom I talked. We came to the conclusion that Louise was: a) being influenced by other women who felt oppressed by men; b) rebelling (but we weren't sure against what or whom); or c) asserting her independence. But certainly she could not be a "true" lesbian; that we couldn't accept!

In December of that year I visited Louise in New Zealand, met her friends and saw how she lived. I found her friends intelligent, talented, loyal, loving and caring women. I found that by being involved in her life I could become more accepting and more able to understand her and her beliefs. I also began to face the fact that her way of life was not going to go away. One of the most memorable nights I had in New Zealand was a particular New Year's Eve that my friend and I spent tending bar at a lesbian dance. It's an experience neither of us will ever forget. It was my first initiation into lesbian social life and it was a rude awakening for me to see women dancing and being affectionate together. It wasn't a world I was familiar with, but it was one I could accept. This year I was in New Zealand again camping with my friend, and we talked about the lesbian dance and all the fun times we have had with Louise and her friends.

Since then I have gone through a period of soul searching and growth in accepting Louise's lifestyle as is. However, this might have been a different story had my husband been alive. I believe that he would have found his daughter's lesbianism difficult to handle and this would have been a struggle for me. I wouldn't want to be put in the middle of them, and though I don't think he would have loved her any less, I think it would have been hard for him at first.

My son, who is thirty-two, dearly loves his sister, but finds it difficult to accept her lifestyle. He is involved in golf, surfing and fishing, and goes about with a group of macho young men. I think that as time passes and their understanding and communication improves, he will find it easier to accept.

I do have uncomfortable feelings when I see Louise displaying affection publicly with another woman, and I haven't delved into why it offends me since I am very fond of her friends. Once when she was visiting home she kissed her lover in front of the house and I felt really uncomfortable. I am aware of the neighbors, and people talking. When I am in Oakland, where Louise lives, it doesn't bother me so much because gay lifestyles are more accepted there. I have decided to handle life with my neighbors and acquaintances by not making my daughter's sexual choice a matter of discussion. I am aware that people probably have figured it out on their own. Some of my neighbors have lived here for over twenty years and I am sure they see Louise as a great person without judging her on her sexual preference.

While I love her, accept her, and admire Louise's wonderful qualities and accomplishments, I still struggle with the outside world of acquaintances and relatives who are prejudiced against lesbian lifestyles. It is hard for me to deal with their disapproval — perhaps due to a lack of courage on my part. She recently "came out" at her high school reunion, and though this is a very small town, nothing has come back to me about her lesbianism.

This year I went to the Gay Day parade, and though I enjoyed myself, there were parts of it which offended me: some of the women on motorcycles, some of the men in women's clothing. The negative parts stand out in my mind because I felt it was a perfect place to show the world how gays and lesbians are not so different from others. I loved other parts of the parade, all the AIDS help groups and the social and political groups. I think lesbians and gays are more concerned with social and political issues — the world as a whole, not just the gay world — than are straight people. I can only judge this by my daughter's friends, but I feel this is true.

Louise and I have a very special relationship. We are good friends and she has taught me a lot. I think we sincerely admire each other. Our times together are filled with challenges, common interests and vitality. I think she desires for me to be as militant as she is about social issues. I understand her zeal; however, I have my own style of concern and action. Rather than by being militant, I find that by showing my self-reliance and taking challenges I can be a strong example of an independent woman. Yet, I also find that by being so self-sufficient I am very lonely at times. The men of my generation do not want an Amazon woman, rather they prefer someone to dominate and look after in return for nurturing.

When I look over the past few years, my life seems to have taken a journey of self-examination and adaptation of my attitudes. I constantly sort and sift through them in order to be at peace with myself. There are still things about lesbians I don't understand, the sexual part for one, and I still find myself wondering how Louise *knew* she was lesbian. But I have had a lot of opportunities to be around many types of lesbians of all ages. I have stayed at my daughter's house, visited other lesbians, gone camping with them. I think it's important for mothers to be with their daughters in their own surroundings and get to know their friends. I think as we mothers find out that our daughters are really in very good company, we can feel better. For me, understanding has come through knowledge plus faith, lots of struggles, and most importantly, love.

Narrow Corridors

A Short Story

by Reva Tow

I continue to pursue my lifelong interest in the arts, creative dance in particular. Photography and writing classes are also current explorations. I live with my husband of forty-five years in El Cerrito, California.

It's been about three months since my mind slammed shut — ever since I realized that Natalie had begun to wear dark pants and plaid flannel shirts regularly instead of dresses. This morning her airy voice floats over the line:

"Mom, exciting things have been happening! I'm so eager to tell you. My friends are giving me so much."

My voice sinks.

"Who *are* these friends, Natalie? Where do you meet them?"

"At the women's center, at the dojo where I study martial arts. And at women's bars."

"Nat, I'm busy now," I lie, "I can't talk. Maybe tomorrow." I hang up, collapse against the cushioned wicker chair.

The disgusting word ricochets inside my skull. *Les-bi-an. Les-bi-an.* Damn you, Nat, you've ruined my life! Mother and Pa's too. We'll all be destroyed. How could you? Maybe we could keep it a secret? No. How can you hide a thing like that? Damn. Damn you for putting me in this awful fix. What'll I do? Where did I go wrong?

You used to be so pert, so petite, so rosy and feminine. Now you're like those aggressive women I sometimes see on the street — drab, masculine. Who are those women really, inside men's clothing? Do I want to know, now, when my child is one of them? What's become of the daughter I thought I knew and understood? At least your father isn't here to be shamed and disillusioned.

For a long time I pretended life was just as usual. I steered my conversations with Nat along neutral lines. With aunts and cousins, my parents and my friends, I dodged the whole issue of Nat. It was one thing to feel my anger in private, but unthinkable to give it voice in public. Mother and Pa would never tolerate such behavior.

Eventually a new voice commanded attention in my head.

"Are you going to shut the door forever, isolating both of you?"

No. I couldn't do that. That prospect was more than I could bear.

I nervously dialed Natalie's number.

"Nat, how about coming to dinner on Friday? It's been so long."

"Mom! It's good to hear your voice. Yes, it's time we got together. This Friday? Let me check, just a minute —"

I waited, tense.

"Friday's fine. What time, six?"

I let go. "Yes, six is good. See you then."

I wondered, what would be a treat for her? What would she wear?

When the bell rang I opened the door and sagged at the sight of her clothes. So mannish — black jeans, gray jacket, brick-brown turtleneck. I hugged her reluctantly. And followed her into the kitchen.

"Mom, you really went all out. Candles, flowers. How neat. Mmmm, what is it that smells so good?"

"Lamb stew. Oh, Nat," I couldn't resist imploring, "why do you wear such unfeminine and dreary clothes?"

She turned full around, her smile gone.

Well, too bad, I thought. I've a right —

"You don't like my new blazer, Mom?"

"It fits fine, Nat. It's good looking tweed. But it's just not soft and feminine."

"I don't feel soft and feminine all the time. Come on, let's eat. I'm starved."

At the table I noticed how well and happy she looked, in spite of her clothes. More like twenty instead of thirty. "Now, Nat, let's talk about you."

Her smile accentuated the circles of her cheeks. "Great. I've really lots to tell you." She served herself a heap of salad from the bowl, poured dressing generously over it and began eating heartily.

"I've wondered —" My stomach tightened, "you always talk only about women. You've mentioned the women's center, the dojo, women's bars — " I recoiled at the words, "and women's rap groups. Why do you spend all your time with women?" And at those places! They frightened me.

"Women are very supportive of one another, Mom. They're less judgmental. I can be myself. It's different with men. They have more power in the world. They expect to be deferred to, to be allowed to take the lead. I don't like that. Women have helped me to know myself, see where my talents lie. I've grown a lot. I have more confidence. . ."

She paused, looking down at her plate. Her blue eyes met mine again.

"I've been a lot happier sexually too with women than I ever was with men. There's a lot —"

"Never mind, I don't want to hear about it." I couldn't. I buttered a slice of challah, took a large bite to stall for time and slowly cut up my tomato slices, thinking that sex between women is too foreign, abhorrent. Where is Natalie's sense of privacy? I would never think of discussing intimate details with anyone else, though I'd admired the male and female body. In anatomy class, drawing class, modern dance sessions, concerts, gymnastics events, art exhibits, the Rodin sculptures . . . very different from two females making love. I took a deep breath and looked up to return Nat's gaze.

"What do you talk about with these women, Nat?" I had visions of secret societies, special rituals. I'd never been part of any women's group except when Natalie was a Campfire Girl. We didn't discuss personal feelings there.

"Mmmm, good salad, Mom. I'm going to have seconds." She helped herself. "We talk about our backgrounds, our families, friends, work experiences, relationships . . . how we feel about religion, race, politics. Our fears, our struggles as women. Not all of us are middle-class or white, either."

I put down my fork. Nat's answer surprised me.

I felt twinges of envy. How narrow my corridor of life compared to Nat's. I did have three close friends, but their lives were much the same as mine. We never ventured out of our white middle-class world. It had never occurred to me to go beyond the familiar boundaries.

"It does sound supportive. But this whole business — I feel a terrible conflict."

"Well, let's talk about it now —"

"No. No, I can't talk about it anymore."

I admired Natalie's independence and perseverance, but I hated all the conflicting feelings she stirred up. How much loyalty did I owe my parents? My relatives? How much to my daughter? Myself? What were my beliefs? Were they really mine? Or were they hand-me-downs from parents, hand-me-downs I'd never examined?

In the ensuing weeks one vision repeatedly rose out of the emotional turmoil: Natalie's glowing face, her confident voice. But damn it, Nat, why did you have to choose lesbianism?

I remembered one day after school, in seventh grade, when I was seated in the kitchen nook drinking a glass of milk and nibbling round the wine-red center of a jam cookie, I noticed a large-print heading in the newspaper that lay on the table: "Homosexual Principal Arrested," and below, "— accused of committing crimes against boys in his care." What crimes I wondered?

"Mother, what is a homosexual? This says —"

"What? Leah, what are you reading that for?"

She stopped kneading the dough. The flour had dusted white gloves on her palms. She looked me straight in the eye and said, "They're terrible people. Especially to children. They should be locked up."

Her lips pressed together hard. Her whole face got that tight look that came whenever I'd disappointed her. I was glad she was mad at somebody else this time. But I didn't understand.

"Why? What do they do?" Why would anyone want to hurt children? A big lump filled my stomach.

My tears rose and flowed over. Another vision appeared: contented Natalie in a crisp cotton dress sitting on my lap as we looked at picture books together. I went to the piano to play Chopin's funereal C minor Prelude. Its relentless pathos echoed my own.

The telephone rang. I lay down the water-color brush. "Hello?"

"Hi, Mom. Listen, I have a great idea. There's a movie I'd like us to see together. A beautiful film. About the lives of some gay men and women. Some of my friends are going. They want to meet you. Will you come?"

She does want me to understand and share her new life. Guess I, too, ought to put out some effort. But to go to a place where almost everyone will be gay? It's threatening — *I'll* be the outsider.

"Please, Mom."

Nat would be right there with me. "All right. Yes, I will."

I paced back and forth across the living room floor waiting for Natalie to drive us to the movie theatre.

When we entered the screening room through the door down front, a buzz of conversations assailed our ears. The place was filled mostly with women, mostly wearing pants. We climbed the steep staircase along the wall, searching for two empty seats.

I was surprised at the number of women my daughter knew. She waved and smiled repeatedly. She stopped to greet a petite dark-haired lady on the aisle. Nat said proudly to her, "I brought my mother." To me, "Naomi's a pediatric nurse." Surprised, I had to admit to myself, hmmm, a woman of some substance. Then realized my thought was exactly what my mother's would have been. The observation tasted like tainted food.

I followed Nat to two seats in the middle of a row, two-thirds back. To the women sitting directly behind, she smiled broadly. Her face flushed with pleasure as she introduced me. The flush warmed me too.

"I'd like you to meet my mother. Mom, this is Gerry and Pauline. Oh," Nat pointed three rows up, "there's Pam and Beverly." I smiled and nodded.

"Your mother!" someone exclaimed on the left. "Wow, I'd give *anything* if *my* mother would come to something like this with me."

I felt like an honored guest. I needn't have worried at all. Nat squeezed my hand. We sat down, and the warmth of touch and look flowed through me like a swallow of brandy.

It happened during my sophomore year in college. Mother and I had set the dining room table for company — the white damask cloth, the flower-rimmed plates flanked by the gleam of polished sterling, the gold centerpiece of chrysanthemums, the wine goblets that glinted in the afternoon sunlight, balanced on slim stems like ballet dancers awaiting their cue.

The performance began when my aunts and uncles and Mother, Papa and I sat down to the bowls of hot shimmery borsht. Mother always became the liveliest of all at center stage. She talked a lot, laughed a lot, used her hands a lot. Her cheeks colored and her eyes glinted like the wine glasses.

The adults talked with animation and sipped the hearty soup. Their loud voices — Yiddish, English, Russian — bounced like tennis balls from wall to wall. Aside from being

Mother's helper I felt unnecessary, unnoticed. Their conversations rarely included me. This time however, the talk irritated me more than ever. They were discussing the same old subject.

"Why do you always talk about Jews? Only Jews? As though we're the only people on earth? The only ones who've ever suffered. Lots of people have suffered." Heads turned, eyes stared. "Why can't we consider everybody? Why should we be better than anyone else?"

My outburst shocked everyone into immobility, like a puppet theatre suddenly stilled. The soup spoons stopped in transit. I quivered inside from my unexpected explosion. The silence boomed in my ears.

I looked down the table at Papa who frowned at me. At Mother. She dismissed me with a sweep of her hand. "You don't know what you're talking about!"

The puppet theatre returned to life. I felt disgraced, obliterated.

The theatre lights dimmed and disappeared. I watched the picture credits flash across the screen. The film was a documentary with flashbacks of individual histories depicted through old photographs, but narrated by each person involved. Then there followed live and current moving pictures of everyone who had spoken. The viewer experienced each highly personal and hard-fought struggle to achieve a life free from pretense.

I cringed seeing the social punishment those men and women were forced to suffer because they didn't conform. They were thwarted, shamed, and ostracized.

It struck me that I shared a kinship with these people. I, too, had spent years disowning the real me, struggling to be what my parents wished me to be.

All the way home from the dance studio on the streetcar I could hardly contain the wonderful news inside of me. Miss Pataky had asked me — me — to join her dance company and go on tour. Think of it!

Ever since I was eight, and Mother first took me to Grace Burroughs' Dance School, it was only when I danced that I felt really myself. Such joy! And now I had the chance to be part of a professional performing company.

I rode on the streetcar seeing nothing but visions of myself on stage, dancing, living with dancers in a dancer's world. High school graduation was approaching. Perfect timing for turning professional.

"Mother, guess what," I blurted out as soon as I'd run up the stairs, let myself in the front door and hurried down the hall to the kitchen. "Miss Pataky wants me to join her dance company!"

"Well, that's nice, but first you've got to go to college." A wave of warm meaty fragrance rolled by as she opened the hot oven and took out the roasting pan filled with braised chunks of lamb. She added peeled potatoes, sliced onions and carrots, put the lid on the pan and returned it to the oven. "Go get cleaned up and you can set the table for dinner."

I really didn't hear her. I was dreaming of being with others who were as passionate about dance as I.

I could hardly wait through the next hour until Papa would come home and we'd sit down at the kitchen table and talk about my new life.

We helped ourselves first to generous portions of salad from the bright yellow bowl and to crusty slices of rye bread and the sweet butter.

"Pa, did Mother tell you the good news about me?"

"No. Something happen at school?"

"No, Pa. Miss Pataky thinks I'm such a good dancer she wants me to be a member of her professional company!"

"How can you do that and go to college at the same time?"

"I don't want to go to college. Dancing is what I want."

"Look, Leah," said my mother, "college is too important, too valuable. You have good grades. You've already been accepted by the university. Not everyone who wants to go is able to, you know. After college, then you can see about dancing."

"Your mother's right."

"Oh, you don't understand. I want to dance now, not four years from now, and here's a chance to do it!"

"No. You'll thank us for it later, you'll see. You go to college first and that's it." Mother was a stone wall.

I shriveled to a pebble. I ate the rest of my dinner without appetite. Mother and Pa talked together but the sounds hummed only faintly in my ears, as if they came from the other end of the flat. I am not going to college, I vowed silently, I am not going to college. As soon as I finished, I ran to my room, slammed the door and flung myself on the bed.

My tears stained the green cotton bedspread. I felt defeated, imprisoned. When my mother came in later, I yelled, "Go away! I don't want to talk to you. I hate you and Papa! I hate you! I hate you!"

Later on, when I went down the hall to the bathroom, I could hear them talking about me in Yiddish. That infuriated me. They always did that when they didn't want me to know *what they were saying. Why couldn't they go to another room and talk quietly instead of switching to a foreign language in my presence? As if I weren't really there. Or maybe I was only a piece of furniture with no feelings? I would never be so cruel to anyone, ever. I splashed cold water on my swollen eyelids and blotted them gently with a towel. I walked back down the hall and slammed my door again, hard. There, that'll show them!*

When the movie ended and the lights glared overhead, I felt red-eyed, drained. Natalie and I exchanged glances, moist ones.

As Nat stopped the car in front of my apartment building, I turned to her. "I'm glad we saw the show together, Nat, but I need to be alone now to sort it all out."

"I know, Mom. I'll call you in a few days. I love you!"

We hugged each other.

"I love you too, Nat."

A couple of weeks later I telephoned my daughter.

"Nat, I think it's time for me to get acquainted with a few of your friends. Especially Esther. You've talked so much about her. She must be your favorite."

"Yes, she is. In fact she's right here. She may be moving in with me."

"Well," I said, trying to achieve resiliency, "why don't you bring her to dinner? Friday?"

"Oh that would be great, Mom. You'll like her."

"But do me a favor, Nat. Please wear that white silk blouse of yours. You look so nice in it."

Natalie laughed warmly. "I'll think about it, Mom, I promise."

The Silt of a River

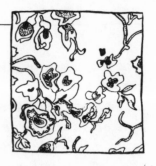

by Jane Allen

I was born in Peoria, Illinois in 1938. I am a psychotherapist, and interested in theater, writing, quilting and gardening. I was divorced in 1975 after twenty years of marriage.

My daughters are lesbians.

I feel good that:

My children are happy and productive people.

Their friends and lovers are also appealing and vibrant people who have added greatly to my life.

They will have children if they choose.

They have been able to talk to me about their choices in life.

I have not lost my connection to them because of their decision to be gay.

I am sad that:

Some people would not like or even get to know my children because they are gay.

Occasionally a person will say something rude or cruel to my daughters and think this is justifiable because they are gay.

One day at a beach someone threw a bottle at one of my daughters and yelled "dyke."

At times, both they and I are fearful that we will be rejected or cause pain when we talk to friends or relatives about their lifestyle.

I have three bright and beautiful daughters. For a while, all three were lesbians. I have certainly had to think about many issues concerning homosexuality. My reactions have been multilayered, like the silt of a river laid down after each spring's flooding. In a way we have been very lucky and our story must be easy compared to some. We each live in cities which have visible feminist and lesbian groups, and therefore each of us has a sense of community and support from other women. Still, there have been great difficulties.

My reactions have varied greatly. Sometimes I have seen their choice as positive: empowering them both personally and politically, raising their standards for developing their professional and personal lives, bringing really nice women into our lives, and connecting them to an exciting and dynamic community.

On the negative side has been: fear for their well-being and safety, concern about not having grandchildren, having to deal with some peoples' disapproval of them for the first time in my life, facing hurt and anger from their dad, and wondering at times if I had done something wrong in my parenting of them.

It's hard work to be the parent of lesbian children because you end up facing homophobia — both directly and through the experiences of your child. Once when we were traveling, we entered a full restaurant in an unfamiliar place in the midwest. A silence fell, and people stared at us, I thought, with hostility. Fear seized me — would there be some sort of abuse? Verbal or even physical? Gay people can get hurt; it happens all the time. Was this going to be one of those times? Fortunately, it wasn't.

Until recently my own knowledge of homosexuality was very limited. Growing up in the forties in the midwest, I knew no gay people. I do remember when I was fourteen, my mother said we should stop holding hands when we walked down the street because a friend of hers had teased her and said we looked strange. She didn't explain exactly what the concern was, but I understood that adult women weren't supposed to be publicly affectionate or something bad would happen.

During those years, my life was strongly influenced by my

mother and my two grandmothers. My grandmothers had both been widowed and finished raising their families alone. My mother and father had divorced when I was about four years old. My mom worked as a nurse and supported us. Each of these three women was dynamic and influenced me in her own way. One grandmother was an earth-mother, the other stood for social justice and love of nature. My mother was a professional woman.

After my midwestern upbringing in the forties, I lived in the San Jose and San Francisco areas in the fifties and sixties. My children grew up in the civil rights and anti-war atmosphere of Berkeley. During that period I knew two gay people. One of my supervisors lived with her female partner. She was very well-liked and accepted by others as far as I could tell. Also, when I worked part-time as a cashier in a restaurant near campus, one of the cooks was gay. He would talk about his male partner in much the same way as I talked about my husband. I rather liked this and found it easy to relate to him.

As my daughters were growing up in Berkeley and Davis, we were a typical happy family. Their dad finished grad school and was on the University of California faculty. Our kids were so appealing that other people would comment that they would consider having children themselves if they could be as nice as ours. Our oldest daughter loved animals, Nancy Drew mysteries and, later, dramatic arts. The middle daughter was energetic, sociable and very athletic. The youngest was an elfin guru, wise beyond her years and very witty. In high school and afterwards they all had boyfriends and relationships with men. The oldest married and had two children.

During my daughters' late teens, their father and I divorced and this was a difficult time for them. The issues were complex and included many differences of style in personal relationships and politics. Like many women, I had at least partially deferred my professional and individual development as I focused on being a wife and mother. I found that in my thirties I wanted it all — to go to college, be more intimate with my husband, *and* have personal freedom. We had many arguments about feminism, which I saw as a request to share more of our lives, including the tasks at home. He saw this as a ploy to make him do more housework, or as a kind of rejection.

Sometimes we fought. Sometimes we were depressed. The girls' adolescence was not as tranquil as it might have been. It seemed as though their father and I were going through our own adolescence. Did we disillusion them about male / female relationships? I don't know.

Our marriage collapsed for good when our oldest daughter was in college. The other girls seemed college bound and had pretty active lives in every respect. During this period, my oldest daughter had a very home-and-family oriented lifestyle, while the youngest went to Southeast Asia as an exchange student. My middle daughter became involved in a women's health collective which provided health care services in our town.

The first to come out was my middle daughter and it was a gradual process. She met and worked with many women — including gay women. I met some of them and thought they were very nice, socially committed and responsible people. She had expressed a feeling that women were more emotionally developed than men. She was living with two lesbian housemates and I wasn't particularly surprised when she said that she had become lovers with one of them. She was already part of a community of women and I wasn't worried about her current situation because she seemed to have a lot of support in her decision and she seemed happy.

Prior to this she had been involved with a young man in college. They planned to be married, but they couldn't seem to agree on how to be parents. He was traditional, expecting her to be the primary parent. She wanted a more equal division of responsibility. Eventually they separated.

She was considering training to become a midwife during this time, and their separation seemed to help her focus more on her career. Her woman lover was supportive of both her personal and professional goals. Emotionally, financially and in the division of tasks, she supported my daughter's ideas and growth. There wasn't the sense of struggle — or the fear that the roles of wife and mother would take away the chance for other things to develop. This daughter is now in medical school and is involved with a young man whom she may marry.

My oldest daughter came out a year and a half later. She had gone from a very active social and academic life early in her college career and marriage to a very inward looking period after the birth of her children. It was hard to get her out of the house.

I was concerned about her development and wondered if she was happy. Her children, a girl and a boy, darling and bright, seemed to flourish. Her husband was gone a lot, studying to be a lawyer. As she began to expand her life again, she got involved in women's action groups, like NOW, and began taking martial arts. She was happy in the company of women and really seemed to blossom. She told me that part of feeling good about herself included advancing the cause of women. She was particularly enthusiastic about women holding political office and felt as though she wanted to work toward the goal of women having equal opportunity in every way.

She and her husband are now separated and share time equally with the children. She has finished her undergraduate degree and is working and applying to graduate schools. Her partner, a graduate student in political science, is also involved in parenting the children. I was more surprised about her decision to be involved with women, but I love her as I always have.

Within the same year my youngest daughter, now a college student, told me that she was also gay. I had wondered many years before if she might make that decision. Her relationships with men seemed a bit off. She never really "fell in love," and kept telling me, "Mom, I just seem to keep breaking men's hearts!"

I hope they each felt my love for them during these transitions. However, with my third daughter's coming out, I must admit I feared other people's reaction to our family. At this time, my ex-husband asked to talk to me about it. He was *very* angry with me, thinking that I had ruined our daughters. I remembered with guilt a debate I had many years before with his therapist, a woman, about the children's independence and their learning to do things like change their own bicycle tires. She said I was going to raise daughters that no man would want to live with. In my own heart I didn't think they were ruined, or that I had done anything to them. Their Dad was upset and angry but, to his credit, he has been able to maintain contact with them and loves them even though he strongly disapproves of their lifestyle. It has been a while now, and he is probably closer to his daughters than he ever has been. Everyone has weathered the storm of feelings. I am very proud of them.

We have passed through many stages as a family: surprise, fear, guilt, anger — and I feel these things again at times. But we finally moved on to acceptance and just wanting to get on with life and enjoy it. I rarely worry if my daughters' lesbianism is a stage, or a political statement, or my fault. I am still wading through my own stereotypes about lesbians. A mixed bag indeed, including that they are particular bearers of women's culture, easier to work with politically, harder to work with politically, have fewer problems in relationships, close out straight people . . . Fortunately I meet enough gay women now so that I must abandon one after another of these ideas.

Recently my youngest daughter and I were on a vacation in the midwest. We happened to be in Chicago during a gay pride parade. There was one group of parents of gays who carried signs which said, "Yes, her mother does know," and "We love our gay children." I was so glad to see them and felt that I knew and shared some of the journey that had brought them to march in that parade.

Our Separate Lives

by Ginger and Katheryn *

Ginger and Katheryn are pseudonyms for two Asian-American women living in a large city in California. Their daughters are friends. This interview was conducted at Ginger's inner city house in September, 1986.

Louise Rafkin: How did you find out that your daughters were lesbians?

Ginger: I don't think I really "found out"; she lives her own life. She was engaged and then she said she wasn't going to get married.

LR: Did she say she was involved with women?

Ginger: Not right out.

LR: And for you, Katheryn?

Katheryn: Well, my daughter was living with a man. She called me and told me she was going to stop living with the man, and start living with a woman. Then she told me she was a lesbian. Now, how were my feelings at that time? I don't know if it has anything to do with it, but having only one child, I think, made a difference. I got used to it, though.

LR: How did you feel, were you shocked? Had you known any lesbians?

Katheryn: Of course I was shocked. I just never suspected that she would turn around and be a lesbian.

LR: Did you talk with anyone about it?

Katheryn: No. I just kept it to myself. I did tell my husband though. He is not one to express his feelings too much, but he certainly did not like it. He said to me, "But what can you do about it?" So we let her live her own life.

LR: Because she was your only child, did you feel a loss about not having grandchildren?

Katheryn: That was on my mind, but that's the life she wants to live. I have resolved myself to never being a mother-in-law, never a grandmother. What can you do?

LR: Did you have any ideas about what a lesbian was?

Katheryn: I knew of lesbians, but didn't know any personally.

Ginger: I read about things in the paper. And I think it has been going on for generations. I think everyone should live their own life. It really doesn't bother me how my children live. She always brings her friends home, for parties and dinners.

LR: What about your communities, or your families and extended families? Does anyone else know that you have lesbian daughters?

Ginger: Our relatives are not that close.

Katheryn: As far as my relatives go, if they do know they haven't discussed that with me. It's probably something they know but don't discuss. I don't know if my daughter has discussed it with them.

LR: Do you know your daughter's friends, or find them any different from heterosexual women?

Ginger: Most of them are professional; I just consider them her friends.

Katheryn: That's how I feel.

* * *

LR: Can you talk about the fear you have about being identified in this book, not that I don't think it's a valid concern...

Katheryn: You say fear. There is no fear. We just want to live our own lives and we want our daughters to live their own lives. Not to exploit them or advertise them.

LR: You are not worried about your friends finding out about it?

Ginger: Not at all.

Katheryn: But it would be best if my husband and I kept a low profile about it.

LR: Because of society's feelings about homosexuality?

Katheryn: It has nothing to do with how society feels.

Ginger: My daughter left home at eighteen or twenty. We have lived our separate lives for a long time.

Katheryn: Do you think that lesbians should be advertised, that the parents should be involved in it?

LR: No, but I know with my own mother there was a lot of fear on her part about what others would say about her. People may feel that it's the parents' "fault" and condemn them. Recently, I went to my high school reunion and I came out to many of my old friends. There hasn't been any backlash about this, at least to her, but it's a small town and people do talk. I can understand her fear — it's something *we* live with every day.

Ginger: I don't think that kind of talking happens so much in the big cities.

Katheryn: I think that as long as there are humans there are two types, those who will talk and those who are open-minded. The way I feel about it is that if they know, fine; if they don't I leave well enough alone.

LR: It sounds like you are very accepting in terms of saying you live your lives and they live their lives. Do you think there are cultural opinions or attitudes that have helped you to feel this way?

Katheryn: It just dawned on me that Ginger and I only have one daughter each. We have to accept them as they are. I think you should also interview some mothers who have more than one daughter.

LR: It seems like it can go either way. There are those women who have one daughter who say, "This is my only daughter; I want her to be a certain way," and those who say, "This is my only daughter and we are family no matter what happens."

Ginger: How can they say their daughter has to be a certain way? You can't change it.

LR: People try.

Katheryn: I think Asians have different backgrounds, different feelings, and different traditions than others do. They are different than American people, from Chicanos, etc. Having only one daughter you have to accept how they live their lives.

Ginger: If you had two daughters, you perhaps would compare them. But that is not my problem. All my children are very independent.

LR: Have you ever thought you might like to talk to other mothers who have lesbian daughters?

Ginger: Really, we don't talk about our children that much to other people. Everybody I know has several children; we don't want to hear about their children, and they don't want to hear everything about ours!

Katheryn: I don't feel that way, as far as hearing about their children and vice versa. However, my husband and I don't talk about that part of her life. We don't say she is lesbian, or she is straight.

Ginger: We just say she is working . . . she comes over for dinner . . . We always welcome her friends here, in fact we have gone on trips with them. I don't say that my son is heterosexual.

LR: So you talk to your friends about them, but don't mention who they are living with, or going with . . .

Katheryn: That's right. Nobody is going to turn around and ask us that, because I would turn around and tell them it is none of their business to ask such things. My friends, they'll know what to ask and that's not something they would ask. I don't think the relatives know, they might suspect it, but I would rather have it that way.

LR: Because you want her to tell them if she wants to?

Katheryn: What do you gain from it?

Ginger: Our friends are not really her friends; there is a generation gap.

LR: You don't think they would have the same feelings about her if they knew?

Katheryn: They wouldn't have the same feelings for *us* if they knew.

LR: Why? What would they think?

Ginger: . . . I don't know, we don't really have friends who are so inquisitive.

LR: And your closest friends?

Katheryn: My closest friend does not even suspect it.

LR: But what would you think they would feel about you?

Katheryn: I don't know. You never ask them, "How do you feel now that you know my daughter is a lesbian?" Would you turn around and ask somebody that?

LR: Well, my mother went to her best friend and talked with her when she found out about me.

Ginger: Our friends, both my husband's and mine, are not that close.

LR: How does your husband feel about her?

Ginger: She is the apple of his eye.

* * *

LR: Do either of you have questions you would like to ask me?

Ginger: What's the difference between lesbian and feminist?

LR: Feminism has to do with politics and fighting for women's rights and equality. Many women feel that lesbianism is something they are born with, and some women feel that lesbianism can come about through being feminist.

Ginger: So a feminist is not necessarily a lesbian.

LR: And a lesbian is not necessarily a feminist.

* * *

Before the tape started, Ginger and Katheryn both wanted to be assured that there would be no way of anyone finding out their identities, and the identities of their daughters. Ginger's daughter, Lotus, overheard the conversation and was upset by the degree to which Ginger and Katheryn were "in the closet." Before leaving the house, she expressed her disappointment to them.

Katheryn: How do you feel about what Lotus said, that she felt sorry for us because of our concern. She was quite disturbed. Why?

LR: I don't know exactly what she was feeling. But I was very upset when I felt like my mother was ashamed about what I was, wasn't proud of who I was.

Katheryn: Of course we are proud of who she is, but not the life that she leads. That is separate.

LR: I think for Lotus, and for me, it is the same. Who we are and the lives that we live are the same.

Katheryn: So in other words, you think if you are a lesbian then you should advertise it and everybody should know, including the parents' friends. The way she sounded, she said that she was sorry for us that we couldn't accept her as what she is. We accept it, but we don't have to advertise it.

LR: If you accept her lesbianism but don't acknowledge it, you cut out a whole part of her life. I don't know your daughter's life, but with many women their activities, their politics and involvement with the gay community is part of their life. I recently won a writing award for my writing in a gay paper. I would like my mother to be able to say that and feel as good about it as I do. Through not talking about it, it somehow feels as though people are ashamed. Maybe that is what Lotus was feeling.

Katheryn: There are certain rebuttals. You're proud, you have said that is what you are. But as far as being a parent is concerned, we don't fully accept our children as lesbians and have to advertise it. Let's say it is bad enough to have a child who is a lesbian, but to turn around and advertise it to the whole world . . . and to your best friends and all that . . . that's another thing.

LR: If we all didn't think it was bad on some level, then it wouldn't be such an issue. What Lotus was saying about being in the book wouldn't be difficult for you. But it is still not a world where it is okay to be homosexual.

Ginger: We accept it, like we accept other things in the world. I accept life as is comes.

Katheryn: But it is not okay . . . I accept her as a lesbian because she is my daughter. But telling my friends, that is something else . . . I would prefer if it were different.

Ginger: Grandchildren!

Katheryn: What other people do is the norm, and I don't consider being a lesbian the norm. But I wouldn't fight it, or change it, or convert her...

LR: You might find it difficult...

Katheryn: There are lesbians who went back straight; there are people who change. Just because you are still a lesbian doesn't mean it can't happen. You say it's difficult but it happens...

LR: I agree, but I think it may be difficult for you to change her...

Ginger: It would be only by her own free will.

* * *

Katheryn: Do you find it traumatic to interview parents like this?

LR: Yes, very.

Katheryn: Because you fear what's going to happen — emotionally?

LR: Yes, and because I think it's very hard to ask people you have never met before about their feelings. I think each of the women I have interviewed is very brave to allow a stranger to ask such personal questions.

Yom Kippur

by Ann Landau *

*I'm an older
Jewish mother of five
and a grandmother.
I have always been a
progressive feminist and
activist. Now retired,
I'm free for full-time
volunteer work. Much of
my activities are with
the Berkeley group of
Parents and Friends of
Lesbians and Gays.*

I was asked once why I gave such high priority to my work in Parents and Friends of Lesbians and Gays. I thought of Yom Kippur, one of the most important Jewish holidays, the annual Day of Atonement. Yom Kippur came about because as a people we think ourselves guilty for the Jews who accepted conversion during the Spanish Inquisition. It was an early version of social responsibility.

Twenty-two years ago a darling daughter confided — with confusion and fear — her sexual orientation to me. At that time I was full of misconceptions and corrupted values. Instead of helping her I increased her pain by saying, "Yes, you're sick, we must get you some therapy." Good heavens! It was our society, including myself, that was sick. Because I let her down then, she had to struggle all alone. It was no thanks to her doctor or myself that she finally won out to a healthy acceptance of herself.

Perhaps in helping today's young lesbians and gays and their parents, I am doing a kind of atonement. My daughter forgave me long ago and I try not to waste energy on guilt. Responsibility, though, is something else. I do believe the saying, "If you are not part of the solution, you are part of the problem."

The problems homosexuals faced were even worse when my daughter came out to me than they are now. Persecution of gays and lesbians was more intense. It was a felony to commit a homosexual act. The most liberal medical viewpoint was that is was an aberration, a sexual preference caused by childhood trauma. Accepting that diagnosis, my daughter struggled against her orientation for years. She had psychiatric "help" and even married. Of course neither the psychiatry or marriage worked. But she tried for a long time to change herself.

My daughter was a third generation political activist. In the 1960's and early 70's, even progressive political movements didn't accept homosexuals. That seems inconceivable now, but then the peace movement, and even the women's liberation movement, didn't have openly homosexual members. Of course, at least ten percent of the activists must have been lesbian or gay but they had to be in the closet. Thank goodness my daughter was strong enough to come through those dark ages to healthy self-acceptance.

With time, I too attained a realistic viewpoint about lesbianism. Once I realized she wasn't sick, that her orientation was normal, the hardest thing to accept was that she probably wouldn't have children. The year she was born, 1945, we began to learn of the mass extermination of Jews by the Nazis. Our whole family, outside the few in the United States, had been slaughtered. The thought that my beautiful, intelligent daughter would not continue our family was difficult.

Also, I love being a mother. Of all the good things in my life — and it's been interesting and exciting in many ways — my relationship with my children has been perhaps the most rewarding. Even as a child, my lesbian daughter had always been "parental" and I'd assumed she would become a mother. I know she would have been a wonderful one. But when she was young it was unheard of for lesbians to have children unless they stayed in the closet. What lousy alternatives! I'm bitter about my daughter and so many others of her generation being deprived of parenthood — and the world being deprived of the splendid kids they could have produced.

For quite a while I didn't think of lesbian / gay liberation as a socio-political issue. I realize now I must have been very dense because I've always been active for the rights of other minorities and women. But it didn't dawn on me that the civil liberties movement should include homosexuals till the Briggs Initiative. This California initiative (which was defeated by a vote of 58% to 42%) would have amended the State's constitution to prevent homosexuals, or anyone who advocates acceptance of homosexuality as normal, from being employed in the public schools. It would have been impossible for homosexual students to get help from school counselors or for science teachers to tell their pupils the truth about homosexuality. It was a loud echo from the 1950's; the "red scare" and "loyalty oaths" imposed on teachers at that time. Only now, instead of "reds," the witch hunt would have been against homosexuals. I campaigned against the initiative, which did not pass. This work led me into working for Parents and Friends of Lesbians and Gays.

My other children accept their sister's orientation. They've always looked up to her. One said, "If she's a lesbian, then a lesbian is an okay thing to be." But my husband died not knowing she'd "reverted" to her orientation after her marriage. He believed, and *wanted* to believe, that it had all been an adolescent phase. He felt such guilt — thought it was a reflection on him as a father, as a man. He never could understand that women loving women doesn't mean they hate men. He never got past thinking that. My daughter protected him from knowing that her orientation was permanent. The child parented the parent. I've found that protective attitude toward parents is widespread among lesbians.

But it shouldn't be necessary. In PFLAG we're working to help educate society to the fact that homosexuality is a normal, healthy orientation. My group is low-key, relaxed, supportive. Many parents newly aware of a child's orientation are upset and confused. The old myths are still pretty widespread. It helps to meet and talk freely with other parents who are accepting of their kids' gayness.

Such acceptance is sometimes hard to achieve. The first step is to get the garbage out of your head. If you have been conditioned to believe that heterosexuality is the only normal sexuality, and that any other orientation is at best sick, then finding your own child is lesbian or gay makes you feel like a bad parent, a parent who has somehow deformed your child. Parents who don't at first have some reactions like this are few. But mothers of blue-eyed or left-handed children don't feel guilty. Such people are in the minority, too, but there is not the social stigma attached to those traits. In PFLAG we explain to terrified, confused, and guilty parents that homosexuality is no more a handicap than being blue-eyed; that nearly all the problems lesbians and gays face are from sick societal attitudes. For many, it's very helpful to hear this from other parents. And we do some surrogate parenting for lesbians and gays separated from their families, ideologically, or geographically, or both.

In our culture, sexuality is an important part of people's lives and ideally, parents should understand, accept, and support their children as they are. The world has become less intolerant since my daughter was young, but still too many parents are homophobic. Too few are like one of the mothers in our group who says, "My daughter's orientation never bothered me. She's a loving person, and isn't that wonderful? Her capacity to love, not who she loves, is what's important."

If only someone had told me that when my daughter was eighteen. We would have both been spared a lot of grief.

No Magic Wand

by Jane Ferguson

I have had a checkered career as a teacher of English as a second language in Cameroon, Yugoslavia, and Willimantic, Connecticut, as a regular English teacher in a community college, a free-lance editor, and director / teacher of a program for teen-age mothers. When asked at a job interview what my life goal was, I replied that it was to find a full-time job with a decent salary before I have to retire.

Parenthood is a crazy-quilt at best, and the task of sorting out my feelings about being the mother of lesbians is a very tough one. There have been many dramatic moments in my relationships with my four children, many guilt trips, many disappointments, but the overall impression, when I look at that quilt, is of bright colors and exciting patterns. And when I think of the narrow, limited person, rigidly sure of all kinds of impossible standards, that I was and would still be were it not for my kids, I can't regret any of it.

I don't imagine many babies have been born whose parents had no agenda for them, for better or worse. First babies, in particular, usually arrive heavily burdened with expectations. I suspect that few parents, when presented with pink bundles by cooing nurses, have foreseen lesbianism as their daughters' sexual choice. I certainly was no exception, and while I think I can honestly say that I have accepted that choice on the part of both my daughters, I have to admit that I would wave a magic wand if I could and provide them with Prince Charmings, rose-covered cottages, and nuclear families, even in the face of all the statistics about divorce, wife-beating, and child abuse. This is where I came from, and what I have, perhaps ignorantly, imagined that I had in my own life. However, there is no magic wand, and my choice has been very clear: accept, learn, love.

My older daughter, Louisa, left home for good at seventeen, and after that there were several years when communication was very difficult. I always seemed to say, or at least suggest, the wrong thing. I don't think that had much, if anything, to do with sexual orientation; I'm sure it was just inevitable growing pains. But having felt very close to her during her early teens, I was really devastated by the change. She told us she was a lesbian when she was twenty, just when we were in crisis with our adoptive fifteen-year-old son. The combination of problems was pretty overwhelming — I felt terribly guilty, a total failure as a parent. I asked our pediatrician to recommend a psychiatrist. When I arrived for the first visit, he asked me what was bothering me. When I described the problems, and mentioned that two of our four children were adopted and black, he started visibly. Then he asked if I had ever considered the possibility that Louisa's lesbianism had been caused by our adoption of black kids. That was a guilt trip I hadn't yet taken, but I was certainly ready for another free ride!

Naturally, my husband and I have given a lot of thought to the question of *why* our daughters are lesbians. As a child and teenager, Louisa seemed to be headed for a "normal" heterosexual life, something that can't be said about our younger daughter, Lindsay, who is also choosing homosexual relationships, though without the intellectual element of feminism. Louisa had high school boyfriends; Lindsay has always had male friends and been involved in "boy's activities" almost exclusively, but the male friends don't seem to have been lovers. Her lovers are female, and what bothers us most is the fact that so far these relationships haven't been revealed to the other parents, who "would die" if they knew. In high school, Lindsay adopted a male persona, and many of her friends thought she was a boy named Bob. This phase passed, and we hope to live long enough to see her comfortable with herself, racially and sexually, and accepted by everyone she loves.

My oldest, Louisa, remembers my horrified reaction to the very idea of a lesbian relationship, when she was in her teens and someone mentioned the possibility of a daughter bringing home a female lover. I don't remember this, but it is probably true. Such a prospect was totally outside my thinking or imagining at that point. Since then, however, among other educational experiences, I have seen my widowed mother fall head over heels in love with another woman. I am now convinced that many, if not most, people have a variety of close relationships in the course of their lives, sometimes expressed physically, sometimes not, and that the sex of the loved one is secondary.

When Louisa came out, there was still a lot of edginess between us. I think I can say that my children's sex lives are something I've been able to stay away from, probably because I wasn't very comfortable about discussing sex with them, even though my own mother was very good at this touchy aspect of parenthood. I remember telling Louisa that I wasn't satisfied with her description of her new lover in a letter — "X and I are lovers!" — because that was literally all she said. We had not met the woman, and we wanted to know what she was *like*. I also remember being very upset when Lindsay went to visit her sister in Boston and was taken to a lesbian bar, at age twelve. I didn't think she should be taken to any bar at all, and I was certainly distressed when she came home bug-eyed about the women dancing together. I'm not a touchy-feely person, which goes with my Puritanism about discussing sex, and one aspect of the lesbian world which I have had a lot of trouble dealing with (as I do in the heterosexual world as well) is open displays of sexual affection.

One thing that has frequently struck me about Louisa's friends and her world is the generally high level of intelligence combined with a low level of formal education. Their eyes are bright, their minds are sharp, but they are heavily into superstition, the stars, reincarnation, their karma, most of them unacquainted with dear Brutus. When Louisa was nearly killed in a car accident (she thought it was her karma not to have accidents, and was careless), her friend flipped through a star book in the hospital trying to discover the "reason" for the disaster. I had to bite my tongue not to ask why she hadn't looked in the book beforehand. While I certainly recognize my own need to approach life and death from a poetic, metaphoric position in order to survive, I like to be able to argue and, hopefully, reason. With all their talent and brains, I wish that Louisa and her friends would work towards taking over the world — but on the whole they are very apolitical, not seeming to realize that things could be much worse, and probably will be, if women don't take power instead of withdrawing from the world. I don't see a lot of difference between the old housebound or convent-bound place of women and this refusal to deal actively with the world as a whole.

One place where our feelings clashed painfully was over the issue of a women-only restaurant which Louisa and some friends operated for about a year. I would not eat in a place that wouldn't serve everyone, any more than I would join a club that wouldn't accept blacks or Jews. The idea of refusing to serve her own father and brothers really upset me. I had to concede that a comfortable "space" is nice, but I think it has to be really private. We thought of a lot of facetious names for the enterprise, none of which the owners found amusing; The Feminist Miss-Steak was our ultimate effort (the restaurant was vegetarian). However, the anti-male hostility of many lesbians is not something I can laugh off; it disturbs me very much, as does the anti-straight women cold shoulder. I quit going to the local women's center a number of years ago because of the unwelcoming atmosphere there. I hope it has changed. I think sisterhood should be a lot more powerful than that. I am also very much disturbed by the practice of excluding male children of lesbian women from occasions such as music festivals, making them stay in a kind of detention center outside the grounds. I feel that is a form of violence against those children.

While I know that many lesbians (and straight women) have a nightmarish past of abuse by fathers and other males, I don't believe that eliminating males from their lives is the way to deal with that pain, nor is it the way to accomplish full human equality and respect.

The biggest and most painful issue that I have had to deal with as a mother of a lesbian was the conception of our granddaughter. Louisa had told us that she and an old friend, who was not her lover, had long talked of sharing parenthood. Louisa had even been to adoption meetings, investigating the possibility of single-parent adoption of a hard-to-place child. We were able to be very enthusiastic about that idea; we were well aware of the need for parents for children already in the world. But suddenly a bombshell: Louisa's friend Marguerite was pregnant, having used a turkey baster to inseminate herself with sperm donated by "an old friend." The father was grandly making this contribution to a human being he had no thought of being responsible for in any other way — indeed, I don't think he even knows of the child's birth. We were appalled, and even more so when we received the added piece of news that if the child was a boy, he would be given to someone who liked males! Having lost a baby myself, I doubted that this would actually occur, but the very suggestion sent shock waves through the family, especially among the male members, and we were all relieved when Teresa turned out to be a girl. We were also relieved that Louisa and Marguerite felt strongly that they should know who the father was, for future health and psychological reasons. We learned that some lesbian mothers use the sperm from several men so as *not* to know the father's identity.

The idea of bringing a child into the world as part of a life-style experiment still leaves us cold. As our adopted son put it, "Why didn't they settle for a kitten or a puppy?" On the other hand, we love being Teresa's grandparents regardless of her troubling origins.

When we responded so negatively to the prospect of the baby, Louisa became very upset and said we had never loved her or her friends. I confessed to having mixed feelings about some of her friends, but I certainly did love her, and I don't think she doubts that any more. I hope not. Her parenthood seemed to defuse a lot of the static electricity that had been in the air, and we all seem to be much more at ease in each other's company. We have always done our best to be welcoming to her friends, even when she seemed to be testing our response. Once she brought an overall-clad woman to Thanksgiving dinner, a forceful person who tried to organize the occasion and who gave unsolicited but very firm advice to all the assembled relatives, and who also left her dirty sheets in a heap on the floor when she departed. For the most part, we have come to like Louisa's friends and lovers very much; I think we have all learned to trust each other.

I can't understand families who close their doors to their children for any reason. We feel very lucky to have our granddaughter, and also very fortunate to have close contact with an interesting group of people we might never have known were it not for Louisa's sexual choice.

We still worry, of course. There had been a lot of chill in our families in regard to our adopted children, and we know that any problems any of our kids have are blamed on adoption. Teresa is bound to have problems, everyone does, and they will be blamed on her parents. It is inevitable that she will have to deal with a lot of pain caused by her "difference" from the "norm." But she has excellent parents, and we're sure she'll make it. We hope they will teach her not only to be strong and confident, but also to accept the whole world without anxiety or anger.

As I look back on what I've written, I'm afraid that my stress on "acceptance" sounds condescending, too much like "tolerance." I guess there are no uncomplicated human relationships. I hope I haven't suggested that I have reached my present position unscathed, without guilt, without a heart full of painful yearning for absolution, for acceptance from my daughters. It's all very well to say that *I* accept *them;* the most obvious lesson I've learned is that I need *them* to accept *me*. I've tried to be as honest as I can about the ups and downs of being a mother of lesbians, but I hope that I have, in the process, conveyed clearly my delight in motherhood and grandmotherhood, even as I have let it all hang out.

A Very Public Statement

by Rheba Fontenot *

I am sixty years old, black, and I'm a very large woman. I have four children. I reared them basically alone. I was divorced, and after spending fruitless time trying to get the child support I was awarded, I finally gave up and did it all alone. I worked at many jobs while my children were growing up. I worked as a cook in a boarding house, a short order cook, hand finisher for a designer dress maker, and a domestic worker.

I only took jobs as cook and upstairs maid so that I would not have to do evening work that brought me in contact with my male employers. I worked as a ticket seller in a theatre. I worked on a ship in dry dock scaling and painting, as a nurse aid and nurse sitter. I worked as a nurse-secretary-companion, ward clerk, para-professional social worker, and research assistant. I sold industrial insurance, electrical appliances. I worked as a surveyor for a psychological testing service. I was a bootleg hairdresser, a paid soloist and concert singer. I baked pies and made sandwiches from my home to sell. I was a seamstress, and when I absolutely had to, I worked a full-time job just dealing with Welfare so that I could feed and house my family. That family also included my mother who was mentally ill all of my life.

I am currently disabled and cannot work. In part this is from a broken neck I received when I was involved in an automobile accident in 1949. It was while I was hospitalized that I learned I was pregnant. Fern was born in the fall of 1950 when I was still wearing a cervical brace.

My dream before marrying was to go to college and major in biology. My father and teachers pushed me into music and toward a singing career because I had an exceptional classical voice. I was born and reared in New Orleans, where I now live.

I actually found out that my daughter was a lesbian on television. Fern and my granddaughter Deborah no longer lived at home with me. It seemed to me Fern had changed personalities over the previous few years. Fern just sort of withdrew from our relationship which had been unusually close. We shared most things including church, social occasions, talking about almost anything, shared financial resources and also shared child-rearing. Fern was my youngest child, my most sensitive child.

I had just gotten back from the store and I received a call from Naomi, a friend to both of us. Fern had asked Naomi to call me and tell me that there was going to be a statement of some sort on television. Naomi suggested that I leave home. I asked her what was going on, but she didn't say. She was at work. She worked for the state so there was very little privacy there. But there was a certain amount of urgency in her voice, and I knew she didn't rattle easily. I took her meaning, and I drove across Lake Pontchartrain where I visit often and where I have dear friends. My friend there was the kind you can be yourself with. She knew of my difficulties and anxieties about Fern.

I was basically informed. I knew that Fern had been fired from her job. I knew that she had moved more than once since then. I knew that she was fired because of incompetency which was not true. I knew that she didn't take it lying down, and with help from the American Civil Liberties Union she sued the state, all the way up to the governor. So there she was on television coming out of the courtroom with her attorneys. I sat there and watched her being interviewed by reporters. She was very cool, very articulate, dressed in a business suit, carrying her briefcase. They asked her if she was a lesbian and if she thought she was fired for being a lesbian, or because she truly was incompetent. And she said it was because she was a black lesbian feminist. I can be calm about it now but at the time I was just about wiped out.

My friend calmed me down for awhile, until the ten o'clock news came on. It was on all the local stations, and the larger ones, too. It was reaching into four or five states.

I felt betrayed. I felt anger. I felt embarrassment.

I am an only child reared by a very conservative set of parents, which made it difficult to accept some of the things that I knew I would have to encounter. I have never been so hurt in my life. This was something I couldn't conceive of happening. My child had chosen this way of life, and had chosen to make her lesbianism so public. It seemed that I was as much the focus of attention as Fern was. I felt like I was being treated as if I had the plague. I became self-conscious about my own sexuality. I wondered if people thought that I was a lesbian. I was made to feel utter and complete failure, that I had done something dreadfully wrong with Fern, with all my children, that I was pronounced guilty with the same breath that they pronounced Fern guilty, but I didn't know of what.

My community's judgment was harsh against homosexuals, harsher with women than with men. Men were accepted or tolerated more easily. But women were not discussed except as curiosities/abominations. On the surface the community was polite, but we knew, we talked about them. They were separate, different, not us, and *they* were not public!

My greatest anger was that she had a child. She did not have to have a child. She had wanted to have a child very badly and was in graduate school when she became pregnant. I was angry that she wasn't married, but she was very cool about it. She had not wanted to be married. But I had such a hard experience myself and I thought about how hard it is for a black woman alone to rear children. I couldn't understand why she would choose this. At the time I was angry about her having the child, though I don't believe she was lesbian at that time.

I was very close to her child, Deborah, and knew life would

be hard for her. I still feel Deborah will face a great deal of difficulty in her life.

The court case went on, and there was continued coverage. Fern didn't call to find out what my reaction was. I went back to the housing project where I lived. The neighbors were gathered around. I could feel that I was being gossiped about. It was very uncomfortable in the neighborhood. I had been in the project for almost thirty years, but it had changed from a very lovely place to one where there was a lot of crime and such. Because we had different values than others there, we dressed differently and some of our social activities were different, it made us more of a target. Criticism came from that segment who looked and said, "They had thought they were so very much and look at what has happened." Fern was a very outgoing person, very charming and sensitive, well liked, and some people were perhaps jealous of her. She had slipped from grace and they pounced on this. Even in the church. I stayed away a long time before I decided to go back. The church is so very blue-nosed and upper crust.

Fern won the battle and not the war. She established the fact that she was fired because of her political activities as well as being a lesbian and not because of incompetency. She didn't get the money she was suing for, but she did win.

We were estranged after that. She moved from place to place, possibly because of the publicity. Sometimes I thought the publicity had died down. One day I was visiting some of my extended family. I was sitting at the counter at the kitchen, and I flipped the page and saw another article and picture of her in the paper. I remember being very angry, wondering when it would ever stop.

Since I am an only child, I felt both relieved and isolated, without support. My family asked questions and insinuated answers. Do you think she was born that way? What do lesbians do? Are there other lesbians on Fern's side of the family? Why did she make a public statement? That was what was so damning, making such a public statement!

Family, church members and others discussed Fern and me. My friends would filter out the hard stuff and let me know what people were saying. It all hurt so much. I did have friends who were supportive and understanding without being judgmental and prying. That was July, 1980.

In November, Fern went on tour with a white lesbian. She spoke and read from her writing, and the other woman performed monologues. It was to raise money for her case, or so I assume because we really didn't talk about it. On tour, she went out to San Francisco for a conference for black lesbians, and she sent me material about the conference. She called right before Thanksgiving and asked if I would mind if she brought a new friend home. Well, my older daughter and son were coming. My daughter is strict Seventh-Day Adventist and very much religious. It was like a family reunion, with all the extended family. There was a great deal of anxiety, and everyone knew that this woman must be someone she was dating.

Well, her friend was much older than Fern, very poised, very stern, very well-educated. She had a harsh, abrasive personality, at least to me. I didn't care for her, and I am a woman who makes friends easily. I wondered whether it was because she was in a lesbian relationship with Fern, or whether it was because I really didn't like her. It was miserable. My oldest son was so upset that he left immediately after dinner. It was not a festive occasion.

During her "friend's" visit, Fern told me she was planning

to move. I had mixed feelings because I knew I would miss her and miss my granddaughter, Deborah, but I was used to her being distant from me as I didn't visit her house much, except to drop off something or pick up Deborah. She then told me she was going to move into her friend's house, and I asked if they were "an item." Her friend replied, "Definitely, we're an item." I was worried about Deborah, who was in first grade, because I didn't think this woman would be happy with a child. Fern said she wanted to go, that it was the relationship she wanted. I wanted to turn the table over, but of course I didn't. There wasn't anything I could do about it.

She moved to California and this relationship went on. I visited the next year at Thanksgiving and stayed through Christmas. I was miserable. I had brought projects to work on and classical music for refuge, but it was hard for me to be around her partner. Apparently I was very nice to her, very hypocritical really, because Fern recently told me that the woman never knew I didn't like her. But I thought she was very bad with Deborah. Some of Fern's other friends were very kind to me, and most were lesbians. I tried to find out from them if my impressions of Fern's mate were wrong, but they also thought she didn't like Deborah. I finally told this to Fern. She understood, knew the situation wasn't good, had made a decision to leave. I visited again, but I don't think they were dating at that point, and Fern had moved away from her.

I had some counseling and tried to deal with my feelings. Because of my dislike for that woman, I had to search myself very carefully to find out why. I don't think it was because of her relationship with Fern.

Fern is now living back in New Orleans and is well-established in a relationship with a friend from graduate school,

Julia, who is white. It was a surprise to me that they got involved. When she wrote me to say she was moving back, she said she hoped there was nothing else she would do to cause me any heartache or embarrassment.

Most of the women in their group are from out of town and I felt angry that I was the only mother who lived close by and had to bear the brunt of the changes in her daughter. I expressed this and pointed out that most of them were from away, some from very wealthy families, most of them white. I know that the white community can be very judgmental about these things, but the black community can be very cruel, particularly within the group of people that I basically deal with. I had a great deal of anger about it. I told Fern once that if she had to be lesbian and live that kind of lifestyle, I had hoped she would not come back home.

Part of her being lesbian is a political statement. She is a crusader. And in doing social work she has seen a lot of women suffer. In my own relationships with men I was very clear about not taking abuse, and I had searched myself to see if there weren't things I had said to her to cause her to be a lesbian. After a lot of searching and some counseling, I don't believe I had anything to do with it. She is an adult with her own choices.

I still very much do not like her being a lesbian, mostly because of Deborah. I keep saying that, but I have to be honest, I don't like it! But I have accepted it.

Fern's mate, Julia, is a very warm person, very kind to me, and has helped me in many, many ways. She is also a crusader, a crusader for civil rights. I accept her. Julia is very dedicated to Deborah and tries to do everything she can to enrich her life and make it interesting. She couldn't be nicer to Deborah than if she had given birth to her. Deborah knows her mother is a lesbian, they have discussed it, and she finds it difficult because of her friends. I think this will get more difficult for her as she gets older.

I live in a retirement center. Most people are older than I and there are mixed ethnic backgrounds. It's run by nuns — one of the most difficult orders — who haven't stepped far into the twentieth century. I needed to be in a safe community, but had some ambivalence about moving here. I was very uptight about Fern and her friends visiting here, she and her mate coming together. This has been discussed, but no one has approached me. Many times Julia comes to pick up Deborah, or do things for me. She has taken a lot of flack from the black people here. It's not just black people who experience racism.

The interracial part is difficult for Deborah. Once when she was getting picked up from day camp by Julia, the kids asked her who the white woman was. She's very bright and sharp and she said, "Oh, that's the maid!" I think Julia was hurt, not because she said she was the maid but because she wants to be considered a parent. But Deborah said to me the other day, "I am very fortunate, I have two mommies and three grandmothers." She included Julia's mother.

Last year Fern invited me to a black women's retreat. In her sharing she made a declaration of love. It was quite an emotional experience. She stated that we had been estranged for about six years and said that she had grown to realize how much she loved me and how much she had angered and hurt me. In a group of about fifty women she asked for forgiveness and asked that we be closer. Many things are getting better.

Ways of Knowing and Not Knowing

by Pauline Johnson

I'm an English teacher in a small city in Northern California. I have two heterosexual daughters, one lesbian daughter, and three grandchildren. I grew up in the midwest and moved to California after I married. I am separated from my husband who has never been told that Paula is a lesbian. Paula and her partner of four years, Donna, live in a small community near the California coast.

I'm not sure how far back to go, so I will start with Paula's childhood. She was one of those bright, organized children who does well in school and has one or two close friends at a time. She has a high I.Q., and there were few tasks that she wouldn't take on. Things she couldn't do she taught herself, like riding a bike or jumping rope.

She dated very little in high school, but in college had a couple of good men friends of long standing. In her last year of college she and Meg became roommates and lovers, though I didn't know the latter for a couple of years.

I have several gay friends and have been an accepting friend and support person to them. When Paula came out to me she said, "I know how accepting you have been of your gay friends. I hope you'll be as accepting of me." She thought at that time that she was bisexual because she had been in some intimate relationships with men.

I guess I had suspected it all for some time. My initial feeling was that she would never experience the joy of having children. When I examined that feeling, I realized it was a selfish one in that I wanted her to have grandchildren for *me*. With two other daughters, one now married and the mother of three sons, I am not bereft of grandchildren.

I told Paula that who she told was up to her. She gave me permission to tell my closest friends. I told her that she should tell her father herself. *She never has. He never mentions it.* She brought Meg and now her partner, Donna, home with her frequently and to our family get-togethers. She called me once to say that she and Alan, a young man with whom she works, would meet me at the movies. Her father asked me if she was dating him. I told him I didn't think so. Since she has never told him outright, I cannot discuss it with him. He avoids words like homosexual, gay and lesbian. I asked her what would happen if he found out now. She said that she would tell him that if she was heterosexual she wouldn't discuss her sex life with him, and that's why she has never felt like she had to tell him of her lesbianism.

As for me, I have found having a lesbian daughter an enriching experience; as her "accepting" parent I am included in feminist concerts she and her friends attend. I sat in an ice cream parlor one night with a dozen women, and looking around discovered to my amazement that I was the only "straight" woman at the table!

I am active in the Presbyterian church, and sometimes that is difficult for me. Presbyterians as a whole are generally hard-nosed about including gay and lesbian people in membership — chiefly because any members can become an officer and, as they think, God forbid we should have homosexuals making important decisions and setting a bad example for the flock!

Another Kind of Different

by Raquel J. *

I am retired now. I had four children and one of my sons passed away a few years ago. I divorced my husband when my daughter Chrissy was about ten, so it was basically her and I. I am Mexican-American, born and raised in San Francisco.

From the time Christine was a young girl, a child really, I knew she was different. Every mother thinks her child is different in a special way, but this was another kind of difference. Since I had a gay sister who had a very difficult time because of her generation and my mother, I decided I just wasn't going to make the same mistake with Chrissy. My mother was from Mexico, very old-fashioned with old-country thinking. I have been fortunate to be exposed to a lot more than she was. She knew what my sister was, but she couldn't cope with homosexuality at all. She had no one to talk to and, of course, my sister did not talk to her either. It was very difficult and I learned a lot of lessons from growing up in that environment.

During those few years when Chrissy was growing up, the adolescent years and early teenage years, life was very difficult for her. It was because of her sexuality, I'm sure of it. I don't think she knew it, or if she did, she didn't understand. I suspected very strongly that she was gay. She wasn't interested in dating, and she attached herself to girlfriends, as do most girls, but this was different. It's so hard to explain; it was just little things that I saw.

When Chrissy was in her early teens she felt like she had to get away from me to discover her identity. I crossed my fingers and let her go. I knew she was too young, but she was going to go anyway. It broke my heart because I was so worried about her. She went to Oregon and I think it was then that she met a lot of gay women who took her in under their wing.

I started getting letters from her, and I got the picture that she was with a lot of people who she could really relate to. Maybe they were surrogate mothers; they all sort of took care of her. She was learning about herself and maybe learning how she could tell me about herself. I already knew this! But I couldn't tell her; I felt she should tell me. She came back a year later, at sixteen, much matured, and she told me she was a lesbian. Of course I wasn't surprised and I told her so. I have always accepted her.

The women whom my sister knew were very unhappy people. I suppose they were going through what my sister was going through, with her mother and with society's view of homosexuals at that time. There was a lot of turmoil, a lot of drinking, and they were very different from the lesbians I have come to know through Chrissy. Her friends are wonderful people and I love them. Chrissy brings her friends home to visit and it's wonderful. I'm on my third husband now, I'm settled, I enjoy life and really enjoy Chrissy.

My husband, David, has never been exposed to the gay world. He's very giving, shy, and somewhat old-fashioned, but if people are happy he thinks that's fine. The ironic part of it all is that his son is gay, too. I talk to his son about it, but it's hard for him to talk to his father. His mother, my husband's first wife, died several years ago and was a totally different person than his father. I guess she never would have understood homosexuality. Maybe God took care of that for him, I don't know. My husband accepts Chrissy, and she and her friends are welcome in our house. What they do behind the bedroom door is their business. Life for all of us would be very different if I was still married to Chrissy's father. I don't think he would have understood.

I feel that gay women have a more difficult time in life than other women. People are coming around, but not as fast as I'd like to see it. People express so many social attitudes that will always keep a gay person down, with jobs, and with children. Chrissy now wants very much to have a child. I can understand it. Most women — gay or not — want children in their lives. I have never been crazy about other people's babies, so I'd just as soon she carries the child. I'm afraid of hurting Chrissy if her partner has a child and I can't feel as though that child is part of me. I want to feel that bond, so I want her to carry the child. At the same time I don't want her to go through all the difficulty of pregnancy.

It's going to be difficult for her. She is in school now and I would prefer that she waits until she finishes to have a child. Raising children takes a lot of time. It's hard; I did it. But that's another part of the lesbian life she is leading. If you are a twenty-six year old heterosexual woman and you've gone to college, you marry a man with a good job, buy a house and settle down and raise children. But for lesbians, it's not like that, they have to do it all themselves and it's difficult, even with a partner.

A Second Chance

by Darlene Palmer

I am the mother of three children, two girls and a boy each a year apart in birth. I love being a wife, mother and home-maker. I grew up in the Congregational Church, studied and was a deaconess in the Presbyterian Church, and now am a member of the United Church of Christ. Since the children got out of high school, I have been an avid tennis player.

L ori was the child I never thought I'd have. I had been told I might never get pregnant, and so when I found I was, I felt God had blessed me. Eleven months later our son Mike was born and fourteen months later a second daughter, Teri.

As the years went by and all the other little girls were having crushes on the little boys, I kept waiting for Lori to find a special friend, but she never seemed interested. For several years she was very interested in being with Carol, the daughter of one of my close friends.

When Lori was in the eighth grade we moved several hundred miles away. At that time I began to wonder why Lori was still not interested in boys, and homosexuality came to mind. I put that out of my head by telling myself that she just wasn't ready for boys yet. In high school she went to all the games and dances, and was involved in band and athletics. She was well known for her athletic ability. Eventually she became very close to one special girl, and I became concerned about the way she had begun to act at home — very hostile, unhappy and removed. It was a gradual change in her behavior and I thought it was part of the teenage years.

One evening I was reading in the living room and overheard her talking on the phone with her girlfriend. She was unaware I was there, and she talked about something that had happened at the principal's office. It sounded as if she had gotten away with whatever it was. Later I told her I was in the room and asked her about what happened. She told me a reasonable story, that a mistake had been made by the school. Later, I felt uncomfortable with what she had said. I debated going to the school because I knew she would think I didn't trust her. It was a terrible decision to make, but eventually I went to talk with a counselor about her behavior and unhappiness.

I found she had more than twenty absences, and the principal and I called Lori in to talk. She would say nothing. I knew she could be tough. After what seemed like hours, I got onto her and finally broke her down. She said, "Mom, I need help. I think I am a lesbian."

It didn't shock me, but I hated hearing it. I felt as though my secret thoughts about her were now part of our lives. She had been cutting classes to pick up her girlfriend, Pam, the girl she had been obsessed with for several months.

Lori went back to class and I talked with the principal about where I could get help. She told me to see our family doctor, and he gave me the name of a psychiatrist. Her father came back after being out of town for a few days, and though he didn't have much reaction to the news that I could see, he said we would give her all the help she needed and was supportive of me.

At the first meeting, the psychiatrist asked me how I thought Lori had become "this way." I thought about Lori's life and all that I had observed and I said that I thought she was born this way. He said, "No. You and your husband have done something in the family home that made her this way." I was crushed. Then he said that because Lori had not had a sexual lesbian encounter, he thought he could change her. I believed him and was relieved that Lori would eventually be all right.

Things seemed to get worse. Lori hated Dr. Brown, and begged not to go to him, but he had said she would do that. I started finding poems in her room, love poems addressed to Pam. I also found many poems about death and dying and told the doctor about them. He said he didn't think Lori would do anything to herself, but I worried about her killing herself.

Once in a particularly bad scene she wouldn't tell us what was going on. She kept saying, "I can't tell you, it's too terrible." I had a strange gutsy feeling and I said, "Lori, are you afraid you are going to hurt yourself?" She said yes, and told us she had tried several times while doing the dishes to shove a butcher knife into herself.

Again, my deepest fears had been realized. I knew how desperate she was, and tried to be home when she was so nothing could happen. For two years things didn't get better. Her attitude was very bad, and she even ran away once. Another time I threw her out of the house because of her actions towards us. I prayed to God to take back this child. Since I could do nothing for her maybe it was up to him to guide her back to normal.

When Lori was about to graduate from high school, we stopped seeing Dr. Brown and began to see a minister from an Episcopal Church. Lori liked him. He said he wasn't going to change her, but try to help her accept herself as whatever she turned out to be. At this time she made plans to go into the military service. She left for boot camp a few weeks after graduation.

Lori spent the next eight years in Germany. They were years that I felt free of the burden, the guilt, the shame, the hatred of having a lesbian daughter. When she came home twice for short periods of time, we could not communicate. I hated her being home, and looked forward to her being gone so I'd be free again. I couldn't feel any love for her, not when I felt she was hurting me so.

During those eight years, Lori sent letters of awards and commendations. She was commended for her performance, her enthusiasm, knowledge, and technical expertise. One said she "exemplified the motto 'Pride in Service.' " Another stated her "individual performance was an example others should follow."

There were also pictures with some of the awards and commendations, one of which I am particularly proud. Lori had been selected as an outstanding military person and one part of the honor was acting as commander for the day which included an inspection of the troops. With silver helmet on her head, the American flag in the background, and surrounded by her personal assistants, she is shown receiving the lined-up troops as they are saluting her.

But when she would anticipate a trip home, I would feel uptight and scared. I told my minister of my feelings, of wanting Lori to come home, but being afraid of her coming home. He was able to help me understand some of my feelings. I began to understand why I felt as I did, and that it wasn't unusual for some parents to react as I did. I felt I had learned something about myself, but had still not accepted Lori or her homosexuality.

Her sister was going to get married, and neither of her siblings knew she was a lesbian. I encouraged Lori to come home to be in the wedding. She came home for six weeks, and things went from bad to worse during that time. This resulted in her not wanting to be part of the wedding. It even got to the point where she left the house for three or four days and we didn't know where she was. My friends noticed that something was wrong and tried to get me to talk about it. They even asked if my marriage was all right. I told them it had to do with the children, which they could understand, but of course I couldn't let anyone know my problem was that my daughter was a lesbian.

One of my friends suggested that I find a support group for whatever it was that was bothering me, and I spent two days calling churches and referral services before I finally found someone who could give me the name of another mother who had a gay child. I contacted this woman who was part of Parents and Friends of Lesbians and Gays and we talked about my feelings and about things she had felt. The key that opened a special door for me was when she told me to allow myself to accept the love Lori was giving me, and then to try to return that love. She said if I did, I would find a very special love with my gay child, unlike the love between myself and my other children.

These were the most positive words I had heard for as long as I had known about homosexuality, and the most important ones.

I started to talk to Lori, though we only had three or four days of her six-week stay to learn about each other in what was to be a new relationship between a mother and her child.

After Lori went back to the military, I started to attend a Parents and Friends of Lesbians and Gays support group and read books on homosexuality. I found myself in an area of life of which I was totally ignorant, but found acceptance in the group and no longer felt alone. I look back at what happened between my child and I, and I know that in those last few days before Lori had to leave home, it was as if I literally held her life in my hands. I could destroy her or accept her love. Maybe it was necessary for me to have suffered such pain, guilt, shame and heartache in order that I might be where I am today. I now understand more of what children go through when they realize they are homosexual and how they must learn to accept themselves.

I felt my hate turn to love; my shame turn to pride, my pain to joy, and my guilt to freedom. Today, Lori and I are not only mother and daughter, we are best of friends. I have been given a second chance on a child I almost lost. For this I thank God — and PFLAG.

My fear today is about the military and Lori's homosexuality. They state that being homosexual is a security risk. It is believed that homosexuals could be blackmailed into giving military secrets because they are not out of the closet, either to their parents or the military. If the military found out about her lesbianism, Lori could be dishonorably discharged with the possibility of prison. My heart still feels an ache for this injustice which Lori must live with each day. She has given nine years of service and is planning on a military career — if they will allow her to serve. And they will, as long as they see her as someone she is not.

The road for parent, or for child, can be filled with hate, guilt, shame and alienation. But that is not the only path. There is also a road toward a special love, a freedom, a pride and an acceptance.

'Winnetka Matron Testifies for Gay Rights'

by Dorothy A. Tollifson

I was born in Wisconsin in 1909, and have lived most of my life in Chicago. I have worked as a typist, stenographer, and an editor, and was even fired from the A & P while working there to make money for college — I never could manage to get the tub butter out of the tub and into one of those cardboard boxes! I married late to just about the dearest man in the world. He died a few years ago and I moved into the city from the suburbs — I love city life. Here it's possible to get about easily at night, and I go to as many theater, opera and music programs as I can.

In the first place our daughter was born without a right hand. Now that was a considerable shock to both my husband and me, and something which we knew we must deal with. We were concerned about seeing to it that this youngster would be able to do whatever she might want to do. Our concerns for her early years were to make it possible for her to learn to do all the things the other youngsters did.

As a young child my daughter had many more young boys as playmates than girls, principally because that's who was around in the neighborhood. As the years went on she had loads of girl friends but was not an outstanding success with the boys. I did not think this especially strange because when I was in high school, many years before, I was not an outstanding success with the boys either, and so I simply assumed that she had somehow been endowed with that particular bit of me.

When she went away to college and came home with a young woman friend, we began to wonder. Also in her high school and college years, she had several friends with whom she spent a good deal of time, and we wondered about these associations. I wish I could remember when she told us, but I cannot. I think perhaps we gradually became aware of it, although perhaps she did actually tell us — if she did, I do not remember it. I do know that neither my husband nor I were shocked or dismayed by the knowledge that she was a lesbian. We knew a number of homosexuals and lesbians, and had known them for a long time. Our main concern was for her. We knew life would be more difficult for her because of this and because of the misunderstanding which exists about these people. We also knew that as far back as you can go in history, you will find homosexuals as part of society, and in most cases, seemingly accepted by it — which may or may not be true as history is always sieved through a particular person. We knew, however, of the misunderstanding about homosexuals in the community in which we lived.

I think perhaps all parents have a dream of their children growing up, marrying, having children, and living happily ever after. I was fortunate in that I had a very happy marriage. My husband is dead now, but he was a man of unusual understanding.

There is a church in Chicago where parents can go for dialogue with others and for help and support. I went to a few meetings and tried to project the fact that my husband and I were not troubled because our daughter was a lesbian. We were having trouble because society comes down so heavily on those people.

I have done volunteer work for many years for a group that works for police accountability. We work with the victims of police abuse, police harassment or excessive use of force. In this work we are aware of how law enforcement people treat the members of the gay community. Because of this knowledge, we naturally were concerned that perhaps our daughter would encounter abuse at some point from law enforcement personnel.

The Illinois legislature was considering a bill to open housing and employment and all other civil rights to homosexuals and lesbians, and I went to Springfield to testify in favor of the bill. I must say the committee before which we appeared was most unsympathetic about the whole problem.

As I left the chamber I was asked by a reporter how old I was, and where I lived and such other irrelevant questions the media usually ask, and I answered him. The following morning the *Chicago Tribune* ran a three-column, four-inch story, captioned *Winnetka Matron Testifies for Gay Rights.*

About a month later someone called me from Waukegan, a city in northern Illinois, and asked if I would appear there in favor of gay rights. I went there and testified. I said that I wanted my daughter to have the same rights as other people in society, that everyone should have the same rights. As I left a woman came to talk to me. Her daughter had told her she was a lesbian and she didn't know what to do about it. I tried to tell her to love her daughter and to accept her the way she is. She telephoned me several times after that and we talked. That seemed to help her.

A good friend, who also lived in Winnetka, called me one day. She asked me about a story which had appeared in the *Tribune* some months before, and I finally realized she was asking me about testifying for the gay rights bill. She told me that she had just discovered that her son was gay and she did not know how to handle it — she was devastated. It so happened that I was going to a fundraising event for some gay issue, and I invited her to come with me. I said I would introduce her to a lot of homosexual men and she would be able to see that they are really very nice and don't grow horns or anything else odd! Well, she came, and I asked several of my friends at the event to talk with her, especially about accepting the fact that her son had told her he was gay. She came away with a much broader understanding of the whole issue. Happily, she and her son are wonderful friends now, and she knows and accepts him.

I have met my daughter's friends over the years and I have formed some very lasting friendships with some of her friends . . . They are all wonderful and I am very proud of her and of what she does and of the kind of a woman she is. Because the kind of a woman she is, is wonderful.

Coming Out
Fighting

by Ann Macfarlane *

I'm a fifty-two-year-old mother of four children, separated from my husband, and I live on Waiheke Island, an hour's boat trip from Auckland, New Zealand. For a long while the island has been in a time warp, but now the roads are being tar-sealed, footpaths constructed, and people are installing indoor plumbing. After getting a year's leave of absence from working in a cafe run by a women's collective, I am now walking for global nuclear disarmament as part of The Great Peace March from Los Angeles to Washington, D.C.

Ana came out to me as a lesbian when she was fifteen. I had thought maybe she was, so it was a relief to me to know. I certainly didn't feel like jumping for joy, but at least I knew where everything stood. At the time I was working with lesbians at *Broadsheet*, New Zealand's feminist magazine, and there had been a rift between the straight women and some of the lesbians.

Ana and I had a good mother/daughter relationship, and that wasn't going to change, but I knew that she had chosen a hard life. I was worried about the turbulent emotional levels that I had seen among lesbians, and was aware of often heavy drinking within some groups. It seemed like a community of women who were critical, judgmental and, at times, unsupportive. I was anxious about all that. Then other people pointed out that perhaps it wasn't much different from heterosexual life. Nothing's perfect. So my feelings on that aspect of lesbianism have changed, but I still worry about the discrimination that homosexuals have to face.

After Ana came out, she was involved with a high school feminist group, and then a lesbian publication. She got involved in a lot of political protests. I was pleased to see that she cared so much about many issues, as I had been involved in feminist work for a long time. Here was Ana, not only following in my footsteps, but forging ahead, and being a lot braver than I. Each generation is going to take us ahead into a better world.

I was concerned because of the violence in some of the protests in which she has participated. The one that comes to mind is when she protested on ANZAC Day, the day of remembrance for those who served in wars. She was arrested at that protest and later in court the cops said that they were going to "get her." That night she got beaten up very severely by some cops who happened to be patrolling a club where a lesbian band was playing. She ended up in the hospital. My mother, who is eighty, was very angry. She came out fighting for Ana; her blood ran cold about it. She was totally on Ana's side and sent her a bunch of flowers.

I was outraged at the injustice of the whole thing. They hated her for being a lesbian. I wrote to the chief of police, and some friends went to see him. We tried to put the case of lesbian harassment to him. We got absolutely no satisfaction from him, although one of the women, who was a psychologist, was asked to speak to the police trainees about harassment of homosexuals in the community.

This year in New Zealand there was a homosexual law reform bill in the parliament. The bill was to give homosexuals the same civil rights as heterosexuals. But many people, and many religious groups, viewed it just as a law allowing men to have affairs with boys. There was a lot of prejudice and little reason exhibited in the debate by the moral Right.

I was active in lobbying for this bill. There were huge petitions by both sides, newspaper advertisements, and involvement by a group called H.U.G — Heterosexuals Unafraid of Gays. Everybody was wearing buttons either for or against the bill, as was I. At every opportunity I tried to talk to people about the bill, and I identified myself as a mother of a lesbian. That made people think about it. They met a nice woman, who had a daughter who was a lesbian — perhaps it wasn't so scary after all. I remember being in a shop when a woman assistant asked what my button stood for. She obviously didn't hear exactly what I said, caught the word "homosexual," and made a critical remark. I was able to say, "Well, my lovely daughter is a lesbian, and she's just like you or me, and I'm very fond of her." She had to backtrack!

After sixteen months of debate, the New Zealand Parliament voted July 9, 1986 to pass the bill. Now homosexuality has been decriminalized and the age of consent is sixteen, the same as it is for heterosexuals. Until then, homosexual activity had been considered a felony in New Zealand. The bill does not ban discrimination in employment or housing on the basis of sexual orientation, as we initially hoped, because the anti-discrimination clause was deleted during the debates.

I worry about Ana. I fear that she could be killed for what she is. She is so intelligent and I feel that if she had opted for a more establishment path in life, she could have been a good lawyer, politician, or something along those lines. Being a political lesbian is not going to be an easy life for her.

A Two Way Street

by Grace *

I'm sixty-two years old and I've lived all my life in Manhattan. I'm a high school graduate; I didn't go to college because I was a dancer. I married very young, and after ten years I had three children. I was married twenty-nine years and divorced about fourteen years ago. I am now in business for myself and am doing very well.

I don't have a specific memory of Vicky telling me she was a lesbian; I think she must have told me bit by bit. She had been living with one young man for about eight years, and after she broke up with him she came to San Francisco with another man. As I became aware of her seeing a woman, I remember thinking lesbianism was merely a phase. I also thought she was probably bisexual, and whether or not that is true I still don't know.

I went through a long period of time trying to understand why Vicky is a lesbian. I wondered whether the contributing factors were parental. I think they are — she doesn't — but it doesn't matter. One is what one is, yet Vicky and I do have different opinions on this. She has said that by taking on the question of who "caused" her lesbianism — her father or myself — we are taking over her life and her choice. She feels she is very much her own person and not just someone's daughter. My ex-husband does not accept her lifestyle; this has caused her a great deal of pain, and me a huge amount of anger. His attitude is totally unforgivable.

I don't go around with a placard saying my daughter is a lesbian. I feel that it is a personal aspect of life. If she was living with a boy named Don I wouldn't wear that on a placard either; it's a personal thing. I find that when talking about her with friends and acquaintances, it's much more interesting to talk about what she is doing than who she is sleeping with. Those are the things you say about people you care about; what they do, what they accomplish, how they live their lives. My close friends know about her, some are accepting and some have offered their "condolences." Casual business friends certainly do not know about her lesbianism, as they don't know such personal information about any of my children. I talk about all three of my kids through talking about what they do. I did find out that my niece, who lives near Vicky, is also a lesbian. I mentioned it to my brother on the phone one day, casually saying that I thought it funny that both our oldest girls were lesbians. He giggled, said something brief and let it drop. I called my niece to tell her I may have slipped something I shouldn't have, and she said he hadn't been able to acknowledge her being a lesbian and that was the first time he had ever admitted it.

Coming to visit Vicky is always a great personal experience for me. I visit her and her friends, and they are always so warm, and so accepting of me. To an outsider, the San Francisco lesbian community seems to be very supportive and accepting. Whatever Vicky is doing, I go along with her, to activities, community events, and to meet and visit with her friends. One close friend of hers called me while I was out there and asked me over to dinner on a night Vicky was busy. And this year, two different women whom I had met through Vicky in San Francisco visited me when they came to New York. We went swimming, had dinner together, and I really enjoyed spending time with these women.

In contrast, I am no longer part of my two sons' lives. There is a love relationship between us, but not a close relationship. I am not included in their lives as I am when I visit Vicky. When I come here I become part of her life; it's such a great experience. She tells her friends her mother is coming, and it's a positive thing — and not something said with a groan. Her friends are aware that I am straight, come from a straight society, and lead a straight life. Nevertheless, I am given so much warmth and acceptance from them. It's been really great for me and I am very grateful for all of it. I believe that lesbianism is not only something that is happening to our daughters, but creates an experience that can be very positive to us as parents. It's wonderful to realize that all the support and acceptance I have received is coming from people who are looking for acceptance, been denied acceptance and yet are so generous in their acceptance of me.

This is something for other mothers to think about; not only what they can do for their daughters, but what their daughters can do for them. If we reach out to our daughters we can gain so much support and understanding. I visit Vicky many times each year and am continually looking for excuses to visit more!

Here, and There

by Juanita Rios *

My mother and father were from Nicaragua, and I was born in this country but raised in their culture. I grew up here in San Francisco's Mission District and later went to college in Berkeley. I married and lived for twenty years in Monterey, California where I adopted two children. I also lived in Acapulco for five years. I now teach bilingual adult education in a local community college.

I have a daughter, Mary, whom I adopted at three months old, and she is a lesbian. She was a difficult child, and a tomboy, and now I see the reason for it. It's a tragic story.

My daughter was very affected by my divorce which happened when she was eleven. She was raised in Monterey, where everything was so proper; the whole social scene was so strict, so affluent and professional. With the breaking up of the family she just went berserk. She rebelled and, though she was very smart, quit school, and just ran around. Unfortunately she got involved with people who are irresponsible, and to this day — and she'll be twenty-seven this year — she's been in and out of jail. It's a very sad thing for me, and I know a lot of it has to do with being so confused and feeling unaccepted. At the time I didn't know what was the problem.

After the divorce she went with her father, who would let her do whatever she wanted. She was away from me until two years ago, when she said she wanted to live with me. In the meantime she was in and out of the juvenile halls.

When I came back to San Francisco four years ago, I realized I had to get myself informed about homosexuality. I am a Catholic, a strict Catholic. I live by the rules, but I don't want to be narrow-minded. I saw a Dear Abby column about homosexuality and wrote away for the name and number of a woman in the Parents and Friends of Lesbians and Gays group here in the city. She was fantastic and I went to the meetings and just loved them.

Mary spent six months with me a couple of years ago after getting out of jail. She got a good job, went to some of the parents' meetings with me, and that beautiful woman inside of her surfaced — for the first time. But she was also in love with a woman who was a drug addict, who had a child, and

Mary spent a lot of time writing her and thinking about her. I knew something was still wrong. After six months she violated her parole, went back to her lover, and ended up back in jail. Last year she came for a month, but she went on welfare, was out every night, and then her girlfriend came here and stayed. My mother was also here and it was a nightmare. I finally told Mary and her girlfriend to get out. Her whole attitude was very criminal and I was afraid. She and this woman left, and I haven't seen her since.

Mary's problem is not being a lesbian, it's more of a social problem. But it all triggers from the very beginning of her sexual identity; she just unfortunately tried to escape and not cope with it all. She has been on drugs throughout this time and I am afraid her mind has been affected. It's such a tragic story. My ex-husband recently told me that a friend of her's called to let us know Mary wanted us to know she was okay. At least she is alive.

I don't understand homosexuality. All I am convinced is that it is something you don't choose. I know that. When I first wanted to educate myself about homosexuality, I went to a Catholic priest. He gave me the okay to go to the parents' group. I don't understand it. It's a mystery, but if God made a group of people this way, they must be that way. To ask Mary to be different would be like asking me to be different — that's a really sound feeling I have about it.

This was confirmed over and over again as I met other homosexuals. I had not known others except my daughter. It was wonderful to meet other young gay people, and older gay people, too. I think it's a lack of knowledge and education that makes people feel so negative, but it's such a struggle because it's so contrary to what society believes. I don't understand it, but I certainly can't condemn it. I just hope and pray my daughter will find her way. She knows I love her and accept her as she is, but it's very painful. I haven't gone off the deep end because I have great faith. I cannot lose hope.

So many parents don't want to face the situation. They try to deny it or live in another world. I meet so many young people who tell us in the parents' group that they wish their parents would accept them. They are so afraid of rejection. I just cannot understand how a parent can turn away from a child. I just cannot understand that. They should be able to love them more knowing that they have a rougher way in life.

I met a young man from Costa Rica at the group, and when I was in Costa Rica I went to see his parents. His mother, who was very religious, refused to accept him. I told her I had a lesbian daughter. She said that he could change, that she absolutely would not accept his homosexuality, but that she accepted him. She said God would change him! It was not a very pleasant situation for either of us.

A few years ago I established a program for mid-life Hispanic women, including education and job options. I was dealing with one woman whose son I had met briefly. I told her I was involved with the parents' group, I thought her son was gay, and that her reaction to my involvement in the group made me suspect it. I called the son to make sure I was on target, and sure enough I was. So I asked her if she wanted to go to a meeting with me, and she cried, she had no one to turn to. She had never talked of it and was afraid to let anyone know. She was really hurting. So she went to the meeting and has grown so much in the last two years it's incredible. She is going back to San Salvador soon and is going to tell her sister. Her son was worried about not being accepted by his aunt. She told him, "It doesn't matter, your mother accepts you." It's amazing how she has changed in such a short time.

I haven't done a lot, but I feel good about having touched a life here and there.

An Open Letter

To Mothers Whose Daughters Happen to be Lesbians

by D. Clarke

I am fifty-four years old and have been married to the same lucky man for thirty years, which seems like a minor miracle. I have one child, and her well-being is probably the most important thing to me in the entire universe. I left work when Deborah was born, and only started to work outside my home again after she finished college. I now am responsible for the operation of landslide abatement dewatering systems. I have many dogs and cats, garden sporadically, read intensely, and dabble in many other things.

T he title of this letter was chosen with care. Being a lesbian is only one factor of a personality and it is something that one is or one is not. The only option for a parent is to accept the fact with courage, first to oneself, and then, with more courage, to one's friends, associates, and parents. That it is commonly in that order is, itself, a sad commentary.

I have one child, a daughter. She is twenty-six years old and since the day she was born she has been the light of my life. There has never been a day in that time that I have been anything other than proud of her. She is bright, literate, attractive, competent, multitalented, has more compassion for people in her little finger than I have in my whole body, and is stubborn, lesbian, and gets bad head colds when her feet get wet.

I suspect that self-acknowledgment of her lesbianism came early on in her life; the announcement to me came only a few years ago, and it came with no great surprise. I probably had much subliminal input along the way, although deliberate speculation on this aspect of my child's life would have seemed as gross an invasion of privacy to me as reading her diary. My reaction was anti-climactic, along the lines of: "Really? Now where would you like to go for dinner?" The surprise was my realization, very slowly, of the effort it had taken her to make this announcement, and her honesty in telling me. Quite frankly, I felt it was none of my business.

There was a fleeting sadness on two counts. First, as a free-thinker myself, I have a clear understanding of the unhappiness which can come from standing opposed to culturally imposed mores. A little deeper analysis told me, however, that this is nothing as compared to the unhappiness of living a lie, particularly to a truth-seeker and lover of justice such as my child has been all her life. The first is a social penalty; the second is mentally destructive.

The second basis for regret was, of course, grandchildren! But even less consideration was necessary to show me how irrational this was. Firstly, lesbianism is an assertion of womanhood, not a denial, and nothing about it precludes motherhood. Secondly, my mother spoke to me wistfully of "nice little families" and the penalties of being an only child, and my mother-in-law was determined that I would have four children, and indeed wrote in her will in that determined belief, thereby fouling up the question of my daughter's inheritance for years to come. Each of them in her own way brought as much pressure to bear on me as they considered safe, but in spite of this I, and I alone, decided on one child. I am ashamed that for even a split second I had the arrogance to presume my daughter should have children to please me. My pleasure in grandchildren would probably be transient, and certainly intermittent. Heavens above, I might not even like them! We are talking about people here, not Cabbage Patch kids.

After my reactions to her statement established me as a fairly civilized and decent person, I began to be admitted to her circle of friends, lovers and activities, and be a party to general discussions. I began to realize why she felt compelled to inform me of her lifestyle, and why it was such an effort, because I began to hear the horror stories. Without exaggeration, that is what they truly are.

I heard of children who were, at best, persuaded to undergo psychiatric treatment and, at the worst, incarcerated in institutions for treatment of insanity. I heard of children who, as a reward for honesty were a) disowned, with the possibility of being accepted when they returned to "normality," or b) disowned by those they loved and trusted most without chance of redemption. I heard of children who were blackmailed by withdrawal of financial support, threatened with heart attacks and nervous breakdowns, all as attempts to make them live their lives by other people's rules.

Bigotry, disapproval, or holier-than-thou patronage from neighbors who might not even be neighbors within a year, or from associates in the work place, is apparently more important than the appeal for understanding and support from a being for whose existence you are entirely responsible. My child apparently feared these reactions, and that hurt, until I realized that it was a result of hearing the experiences of others.

To withdraw financial and emotional support from a child just trying to make that final step into total independence, to apply pressure by threatening illness, to induce self-doubt and imply mental instability at an age when introspection and lack of experience lends credence to the charge; all this adds up to psychological abuse, whichever way you choose to look at it. Am I reaching any of you out there? I am a mother of an only daughter, married to the same man for thirty years, in other words a card-carrying member of your own union, and I am telling to that this behavior is inexcusable, and it is ugly. Sometimes an attempt is made to justify these reactions on the basis of concern for the child's future and happiness. It is very hard to see how such behavior translates into concern for the happiness of a child who is taking her courage in both hands and asking for love and support.

Take a look at your lesbian child on this basis: you can lie to your child, your neighbor, or your psychiatrist, but you cannot successfully lie to yourself. What is so lacking in your life that you need to achieve total control of another person to feel fulfilled? Or, why is your ego so frail that only total control and obedience can assure you that you have any value? Or, whence springs an insecurity which can only be assuaged by the knowledge the whole world is marching in lockstep to your drum? These are good questions to start with. The dominant question is, however: When did society's opinion or approval become more important to you than the chance for happiness for your own child? Listen to her and believe, however hard it may be for you, that she knows better than you do what makes her happy or unhappy. As a person she has a right to make her own decisions, and as your child she has the right to expect your support.

Generations

by Merle Woo *

I am Chinese and Korean-American, forty-four, and an ex-lecturer at the University of California at Berkeley. I'm a socialist-feminist and a member of Radical Women and the Freedom Socialist Party. In 1982 I was fired for supporting student democracy, being a member of a political party, and teaching about racism, sexism, heterosexism and politics in the classroom. I sued on the basis of discrimination and though I won reinstatement and a two year contract, I am again fighting for my job.

I am a lesbian. When I told my own mother she just sat there and was still. It was dark and she just sat there in the dusk. Finally she said, "I hope you can give me something to read because I don't know anything about it." A couple days later I brought her some things to read. I think during this time she was in shock. Still in a state of shock she read a few things, but then as it sunk in she got mad. She was furious. I was thirty-seven then, and she was about seventy.

She has always internalized oppression, whether it was racism or sexism or things she faced working as a domestic. So she blamed herself for my being a lesbian. She thought it must have been her fault because she was a lousy parent, or because of something my father did. For the first two years I didn't see her much. I thought, "I am being discriminated against at work, and everywhere, why should I go and be discriminated against by my own family?" — because she censored that whole area of my life. But after all these years, it must be nearly eight now, she has slowly come around. For the first time, she has asked my lover to come over and have lunch. She still doesn't forgive me for the years I stayed away, but she has opened up some since then.

Now, my mother doesn't know about my daughter, Emily, who came out as a lesbian two years ago. When I told Emily about my lesbianism she was twelve, and she said to me, "I think everyone's bisexual and it's society that makes you go one way or another." She hasn't had any problem with it. I think it's good to have a parent who is out as a lesbian or gay parent, because it gives children a chance to realize there is a choice.

I wasn't too surprised when she came out to me. I think maybe it was her independence, and her feminism — although that doesn't mean straight women are not feminists

— but she never got involved with boys, going steady or any of that. In a way I agree with Emily's first response, that sexuality is a huge spectrum and that it's society that imposes rigid standards. It's very connected with sexism, because if there was real equality between men and women it wouldn't matter who you loved, or with whom you made love. In a lot of tribal cultures there isn't even a word for homosexuality because it doesn't matter.

For my mother, I think it's her Asian culture that has made her so homophobic. I remember growing up she couldn't say the word homosexual. She was brought up in a missionary home here in America, so there are layers of sexism, of self-negation, and of serving everyone. In spite of that self-negation she is one of the strongest women I have ever known. Also, part of it is that she didn't have a political perspective. Because she is so isolated she can only see herself as an individual, and holds herself responsible for everything that happens to her. But if she could see how cultural values have affected her, she could see that they could change. Not that she wouldn't love her Korean culture, or my father's Chinese culture, but that she could see culture as something dynamic and changing.

It wasn't until I came out as a radical — a socialist-feminist — that I was able to come out as a lesbian with no guilt whatsoever. I could see how patriarchy and monogamy and private property have affected the attitudes of society; as I said, in collective societies no one cares about homosexuality. My daughter benefits from seeing these connections, she doesn't feel any guilt about her lesbianism, but sees herself in a political perspective. She fights for lesbian and gay rights while fighting for racial equality and all the rest of it. As she says to me, "I don't have to be Asian on Monday, a lesbian on Tuesday, a woman worker on Wednesday," and so on. It sure is better this way, and makes one more healthy mentally. Suppose there's a whole lot of us who are totally happy with ourselves and we offer a real alternative way of living. And then we point out the real oppression of the family and of sexism in this society. Then we become really threatening.

I just got fired for the second time by the University of California at Berkeley. My contract was finished and they said they never had any intention of keeping me on. I was not treated fairly and am now fighting again to get my job back. People wonder why it's always me and not other radicals. There is a big difference between someone who only talks about racism, and someone who really challenges the status quo. I think that lesbians, lesbians of color, and radical lesbians of color really threaten the status quo and the university system as well. We threaten every single real rigid institutional structure. The university itself is racist and sexist and is teaching people how to be cooperative workers for corporate America, or managers who put other people down. I remember when I first got out of university I was an intellectual elitist! I was ashamed of my mom, ashamed of my dad because he spoke broken English and was just a butcher in a grocery store. That's not the way to learn, not the way to be. We need to turn the whole structure on its head.

I think that this book is about generations, about how issues get spread out. We have a lot of work to do, to keep up the challenge to the nuclear family. Although we can liberate ourselves personally in many ways, accept ourselves and live happily, it's necessary to keep that in a context of how we can really change society. The nuclear family is the cornerstone of capitalism. Sexism and the use of women and their labor, and the way kids are treated in this society, all of that we challenge because we are lesbians. I am very happy to be gay, and to be part of that challenge.

Taming the
Devils Within

by Diane Rae

*I'm a forty-nine-year-old
Jewish woman, born
and raised in Chicago.
My parents were born in
this country, and my
grandparents came from
Russia / Poland and
Alsace-Lorraine. I've
been divorced for eight
years and am a realtor in
Scottsdale, Arizona. We
have no religious
affiliations currently —
religion was never on
our list of priorities.
Both my daughters are
college graduates. I
wish I were as well!*

My daughter's pronouncement, when she was twenty-two and in college, was the culmination of years of disquieting, unspoken dread. There were no specific reasons why I began to suspect her homosexuality from a very early age, but I did, as early as when she was six or seven. These thoughts were not actually at a conscious level, but whenever they started to surface I felt threatened and quickly suppressed them. I would start to concentrate on how pretty she was, how feminine and attractive, albeit she was a "tomboy" and loved to play ball with the boys. She was much less passive physically than girls tend to be, and we were proud of her athletic prowess and achievements.

During her growing years before high school, her closest friends were usually boys and she had great difficulties making girlfriends. She felt an indefinable hostility from them, and she became lonely and self-conscious. She used to cry and ask why she was "different" than the other girls. I remember a particularly poignant time when she and I were having one of our soul-searching talks and she said, "It seems I have to be someone different for every girl I'm with . . . I don't know what they want me to be, but I feel like I have to be what they want me to be. It's making me so tired." She was only about twelve or thirteen at the time.

In high school she began to meet new people and formed some friendships that have lasted through to the present. They were very intense, and so infused with a quality of desperation that my suspicions overcame my reticence and I hesitantly and clumsily asked her if she perhaps ever had "unusual sexual fantasies or thoughts" that were bothering her. Her response was to laugh it off as an absurdity, which I found very reassuring.

For three more years I ignored my own inner voices while she continued to date boys on an occasional basis, and partied a lot with her girlfriends. The summer she graduated from high school she came to me one night and in a rather controlled panic, poured out a confession to having had a homosexual affair during spring break with a good friend's older, married sister. She was frightened and needed reassurance — and so did I! but my main concern was that she not judge herself too harshly and do something rash such as attempt suicide. So I tried to convey my love, and to suggest that she was young and experimenting sexually — a natural thing to do.

Another three years or so passed and then one night she called long distance from college and dropped it on me like a ton of weight. She was gay, she was sure of it, she had accepted it, and so must I. She also insisted there was no reason for me to feel guilty, or to try and lay blame anywhere. But of course I knew otherwise! I could recite a whole litany of things my ex-husband and I had done wrong. Then I cried for having made her life more difficult, for the grandchildren she would never give me, for my imagined humiliation before family and friends.

Luckily, my mourning period was short-lived. I began to read up on homosexuality. I called a psychiatrist friend and discovered most of my fears were selfish and unfounded. Mainly, I quickly understood that she needed my love and support more than ever before, and that she was still the same person I'd loved before. She was not suicidal, promiscuous or sick. I realized how hard it was for her to face her own truth and how lucky I was that she trusted me enough to confide in me, despite the possibility of rejection.

Each mother who has had to come to terms with her

daughter's lesbianism probably feels, as I did, that her situation is somehow different . . . that her problems are special. There are parts of each story that are unique. In my case, I blamed my behavior during my daughter's formative years — between two and five — the time after her sister was born. I was troubled and immature, and a potentially abusive parent, and I resorted to spanking her too frequently. Luckily, I got help through psychotherapy and that bomb was diffused quickly, but I always carried with me the guilt of those early years. My sixth sense was constantly watching for signs that I had sown the seeds of her problems by my own mistakes. Her admission was the confirmation of this fear.

I now believe the homosexual dynamics are probably a natural process occurring before birth, and that she would be a lesbian in spite of my actions, but every now and then that ogre raises its ugly head and gives me a moment's pause.

She has come out at work, with old friends, and now, with her father, my sister and nieces. The only two people she has intentionally not told are my parents, whom she loves dearly and thinks would be painfully confused about her lesbianism. She believes that they already sense it, but if they wanted to cope with it on a conscious level that they would ask why their lovely twenty-eight-year-old granddaughter never dates men.

Her younger sister was not really surprised, nor upset, although for a few years she thought the gay lifestyle was weird and strange. Her judgment has mellowed with time. They are closer than ever before and have even bought a home together as neither has a permanent relationship with anyone special at this time.

My primary personal devils to contend with and overcome

were based upon the misinformation and mythology that abounds about gay children, which leads to guilt feelings and defensiveness. She came to that bridge and crossed it by herself, before helping me to the other side. She pressured me into seeking out some kind of group to share my doubts and fears with, and by a sheer stroke of dumb luck I discovered Parents and Friends of Lesbians and Gays. It only took one meeting for me to regain a healthy perspective about myself as a mother of a gay daughter. I wish all parents could stop torturing themselves — as I did — with self-recriminations that only serve to widen the distance between them and their children.

A Family
of Four

by Louise *

*I am a fifty-one-
year-old mother of
three lesbian daughters.
I am also a lesbian.
I was married for
thirteen years to a man
who was thirty years
older than me.*

I wasn't really aware of my youngest daughter's lesbianism for quite some time. She told me about it, but at the time it didn't really register. She was living in Israel and I wasn't very connected to her life then. She came home for a visit and mentioned that she had a woman lover, but I didn't think about it much after she went back.

Next, my middle daughter, who was twenty-one at the time, brought her lover with us on a trip we took to Lake Tahoe. I didn't actually know she was her lover at that point, but I knew that the other woman was gay. I finally asked her if they were together and she told me they were.

It all started to register. Yet I found I really liked her lover, and I thought it was great that they were together. Together they were really fun. The youngest daughter was still traveling and I thought at that time lesbianism was just something she was going through.

Then my oldest daughter, who had been told about her younger sisters, said she was "going around" with a woman. So, again, I asked if they were lovers and she said yes. She wondered why it took her so long to tell me because both her little sisters had already managed to come out to me! That was about five years ago, when the oldest was twenty-five.

I never thought their lesbianism was anything I did. I've never read any books on lesbianism, but I just don't worry about the why of it. I was a working single parent from the time the kids were in their early teens. I had a relationship with a man, but it wasn't live-in. I, myself, grew up in a very open household. My father was a minister and a pacifist and my mother was in the Women's International League for Peace and Freedom in World War I. They were both missionaries, and my father counseled conscientious objectors in World War II. My mother did the same during the Vietnam years. I grew up in a loving, and forgiving, Christian home — in the true sense of the word Christian. My parents weren't fire and brimstone Christians, but people working for peace and civil rights.

I had a sexual experience with a woman in 1968 when I was breaking up with my husband. It was a "one-night stand" with my neighbor. At the time, my life was pretty devastating. The affair was only a one-night thing, but when my daughters started coming out to me, I understood it thoroughly.

I was visiting one of my daughters and her lover a few years ago when I finally came out. I had been thinking about it for a long time and thought I was ready. A woman came on to me while I was visiting and we got together. My daughter was pretty angry with me because she knew the woman and didn't think she was right for me! The affair was short-lived.

That affair opened it all up. I started to go to women's dinners and events, and went out with several women. Then I met Barb, my current lover, and that was it. She was also a friend of one of my daughters. We fell in love and are still living together today, years later.

Purple Balloons on Market Street

by Constance Shepard Jolly

I was born to medical missionary parents in Istanbul, Turkey, where I lived at various periods of my life, and where I met my husband. I went to Wellesley College, and much later, to the University of California at Berkeley for a Master of Arts degree in Near Eastern Studies and a Master of Library Science degree. Since 1978, I have worked as a fundraiser with the American Friends Service Committee in San Francisco.

About noon on June 26, 1983, my husband and I received a standing ovation from a cheering crowd of a quarter of a million. Men and women ran out from the sidelines of the crowd to embrace us and to thank us. The air was full of balloons, marching band music, exuberant joy, and overwhelming love, much of it directed toward Bob and me. Yet only a dozen or so in the crowd knew our names. And it was hardly the kind of success story I could have written about to my college class secretary to put in the alumnae notes.

Twenty-five years ago I did write to the class secretary, proudly asking her to announce the birth of our first child, Margarett. I wanted all my classmates to share my joy. I dreamed that she would grow up bright, good, successful, go to college, marry an equally good, bright, and successful man, and have children.

This was the pattern in the family where I was the youngest of five, and I assumed it was the only pattern of fulfillment for a woman. But the intervening quarter-century has taught me a rich diversity of patterns and Margarett has been one of my principal instructors.

The June 26 extravaganza was, in fact, a celebration of our pride in Margarett, as Bob and I walked in the San Francisco Lesbian and Gay Freedom Day Parade along with ten other middle-aged men and women under a banner that read "Parents and Friends of Lesbians and Gays." I wasn't prepared for the crowd's enthusiasm. At first, it made me quite shy. Then of course I began to enjoy the applause. And finally, I was deeply moved that parents publicly demonstrating their love for their homosexual children was, to the gay men and lesbians in that vast crowd, a cause for cheering, clapping, and often tearful gratitude.

We wished Margarett and her lover Helen could have been there with us. But they live in New York City and were participating in the Freedom Day Parade there.

I shall never forget the summer of 1976, the year Margarett graduated from high school. Our family was attending a church conference and one hot afternoon, Margarett plopped down beside me on the sleeping bag where I was resting, and after a long pause said, "Mom, have you noticed that I'm not around when there is a lesbian interest group scheduled?"

It was my turn to be quiet for a long time. I'd been picking up hints from friends of Margarett's that her relations with some girls were more than casual. One classmate had said something about "Margarett and the other dykes." And the mother of another had said of Margarett's high school that it was a difficult place for lesbians.

During her last two high school years, some of Margarett's attitudes and actions had puzzled Bob and me — having her head shaved, for example; getting a turkey tattooed on her shoulder; not wanting to spend more than thirty-six hours at home during vacation. I'd tried to accept that her restlessness was normal adolescent development, but in a family that prizes honesty and closeness, it troubled me. When the references to homosexuality began to be unmistakable, I decided to ask her outright. Her confession in the form of that question saved my asking.

My initial worry was that Margarett would wish that she were a boy. So I asked her if she was happy about being a lesbian and if she was glad to have a woman's body. She looked at me with such directness and answered "yes" with such conviction that I was reassured on that score.

For at least two more years, though, I found myself wondering if she should have psychiatric counseling, or if we should, and if there had been serious mistakes in the way we had brought her up. I wondered if she had had some traumatic, scarring experience with a man. Or been seduced by an older woman. Or gotten stuck in a preadolescent crush phase.

I was worried about the effect on our younger children. In a conversation with Margarett and Chris, who was the first woman to stay overnight in our house after Margarett had "come out," I begged them to be discreet, especially in front of Margarett's little sister, Catherine, who was then fifteen. I'm not sure what it was I feared, that she'd "catch lesbianism"; that she'd ask me questions I couldn't answer, or what. Maybe I just wanted them to be so discreet that none of us would have to acknowledge what we had been told and could go on pretending that nothing had changed. Anyway, Margarett pointed out to me that months before she'd dared tell Bob and me, she'd told her brother and sister her "secret." I was left with my own discomfort and no younger children to "protect."

In my early discomfort, I didn't know anyone I could talk to. Mostly Bob and I avoided the subject. We didn't know how to talk about it to each other, or even how to think about it ourselves. Bob now says that he used to have the standard American male prejudices against homosexuality. And we didn't know any other parents in our circumstances, or thought we didn't.

I resorted to reading, and unfortunately I was too shy, or too ashamed, to ask for guidance in my choice of books. I should have asked Margarett. She would probably have been pleased at my interest in becoming better informed, and she would surely have given me good recommendations. As it was, I tried to find what I could, and I looked in the wrong places.

In a religious bookstore I found a book written by a woman psychiatrist. Here, I thought, would be the ultimate authority. That was five years after Margarett had told us about her lesbianism. She was already living in New York, supporting herself as a printer. I was on my way to visit her for the first time, and I'd taken the book along to read on the plane. This particular psychiatrist's thesis was that lesbians are endlessly searching for the love their mothers denied them in infancy. I was stricken! I began to sob so copiously that the passenger next to me asked me if something was wrong.

What could I say? "Yes, I've just found out that I've done something awful to my daughter." "No, no. I always cry over novels."

Behind my fear of what I might have done to Margarett there still lingered the prejudice that something is wrong with a person who is in love with someone of the same sex.

I continued to look for clues that would explain how my daughter could deviate so far from an established family pattern. I carefully reviewed Margarett's life up to that point. She was the first child, a treasured delight to Bob and I. Being the youngest in our respective families, we had several nieces and nephews each by the time we were married, and we both loved first the idea and then the fact of being parents. When Margarett was sixteen months old, Paul was born, and two and a half years later, Catherine. My attention, if not my love, had surely been diverted from Margarett at an early age. But this is true in every family, and not every oldest girl is a lesbian!

I looked at family pictures and studied Margarett as a baby and a little girl. I saw a child who was bright, alert, independent, somewhat competitive, funny, occasionally secretive. She had a firm mouth and an erect posture that said, "I know what

I want and it would probably be a good idea not to interfere too much in my getting it."

She liked school and did very well. She was conscientious and determined, and as she went along, mastered several skills, mostly by teaching herself and practicing over and over until she was satisfied. Occasionally, she would ask for instruction, but only as much as she felt she needed. She taught herself to roller skate, then to ride a bicycle, spending hours and hours by herself until she'd become expert. I think that this self-instruction gave her confidence to realize that she could learn by herself whatever she needed to know.

I think it is fortunate that, being the innovative groundbreaker she is, Margarett has this confidence and independence. During the first couple of years that Bob and I knew of her lesbianism — that period of time when we feared that something was wrong with her — we might have tried to change a more malleable child. And we might have done her and ourselves great harm.

I finally realized that searching for explanations for what made Margarett a lesbian was getting me nowhere. When I stopped looking for an answer in the past, within myself, and in books, and started looking, really looking at who Margarett is, I saw a young woman with whom I could find little fault.

She is not sick. Neither physically nor psychologically nor morally. She is competent, mature, confident, considerate, and most of the time, happy. She has the spare, strong build of a gymnast, a terrific sense of humor (no one can make me giggle as she does), a fiery sense of justice, good mechanical skills, and an intelligent curiosity that keeps her reading and learning though her formal education stopped after high school.

Margarett and Helen have lived together for six years. They have transformed the apartments (two, now) that they could afford from filthy, dingy New York tenements to cheerful, comfortable homes.

How to tell the extended family about Margarett's lesbianism has been tricky. I wanted them to know her as a complete person before knowing just this one aspect of her life. One of the last to know was my ninety-year-old mother. One day last summer, I visited her and took her for a drive. As we drove along, Mother asked, "Do Margarett or Catherine have boyfriends?"

I decided to plunge in. Mother had met Helen earlier that summer when the girls and I had stopped by at her nursing home. When she met Helen she said, "And this is Margarett's Helen!" So I thought it was going to be easy. But Mother didn't know, or had forgotten the vocabulary. Words like lesbian and homosexual she said she didn't understand. Finally I said, "Mother, Margarett and Helen live together as a couple. They give one another the same kind of love and support that a married couple do." And Mother said, "Ah, that I can understand!" Mother had, in a few moments, made the leap that took Bob and I two or three years.

For us it wasn't a leap but a gradual process of understanding, appreciation, and acceptance. And now we've stopped looking for explanations, realizing at last what caused Margarett to be homosexual is unknown and probably unknowable. It is as irrelevant as what caused Paul to be left-handed, Catherine to have freckles, or, for that matter, her parents to be heterosexual.

While Bob, as I said, acknowledges that he used to have the traditional American male prejudice against "queers," he became active in supporting gay rights long before I did.

In 1978, voters in California were asked to vote for the Briggs Initiative, which would have barred from the classroom any teacher who was homosexual or advocated gay rights. Bob, a public school teacher who was active in the civil rights movement and in the peace movement during the Vietnam War, hit the streets again, marching with Margarett in Sacramento to protest the initiative. Later that summer he walked in the Gay Freedom Day Parade.

Thanks to the hard work of many volunteers and the innate good sense of the California electorate — at that time at any rate — the Briggs Initiative was defeated. Bob hasn't missed a Gay Freedom Day Parade since.

Bob and I have become increasingly aware of the extent to which homosexual men and women have been oppressed. Margarett often wears a pin with a pink triangle on a gray circle. I had thought of it as merely an attractive design until she told me that it was the emblem homosexuals were forced to wear in Nazi Germany, just as Jews had to wear a yellow Star of David. I learned that the jocular-sounding term "fag" or "faggot" is not so funny when one realizes its origins — homosexuals burned at the stake in the Middle Ages. In fact, the language and humor of homophobia, like any ethnic slur, cease to be acceptable when one has felt their impact and pain.

When Bob and I realized that many gay men and lesbians we know are not able to talk to their parents about something so central in their lives as the person with whom they are in love, and that many parents are in deep personal anguish over having a homosexual child, we decided to do what we could in our community.

We discovered Parents and Friends of Lesbians and Gays and located the group in our area. We organized meetings in our own community. The structure is informal and we are listed with the local Gay Information Switchboard so other parents can find us. A nearby Lutheran church has offered us the use of their facilities. Often young gay men and lesbians come to meetings to be with accepting adults. They are very helpful to us parents who want and need further education.

A concern that often arises in the parents' group is the question of grandchildren. Interestingly enough, it is usually the fathers who feel most keenly the deprivation of not having grandchildren. Bob is no exception. He delighted in our children and is eager now for grandbabies. But Paul was married this summer and his wife has a five-year-old daughter. Bob and I are enjoying "instant" grandparenthood. Moreover, we know three lesbian couples who have chosen to have children, so it is possible for parents of homosexual children to still be grandparents. Bob and I have also talked of taking in foster children after we retire. There are many ways to express the longing to enjoy small children.

A very positive development is that churches are beginning to recognize their obligation to counsel gays and their families, and to have support groups for them within the church. The religious community has a special responsibility, it seems to me, to consider the biblical misinterpretation of homosexuality as "sin." My own religious conviction is to look to the inner dictates of the spirit for moral guidance. On the other hand, my upbringing and my early Bible study gave me a deep respect for the Bible. I find in Biblical teaching overwhelming persuasion on the side of love, tolerance, and affirmation of life. Jesus' harshest words are against hypocrisy. Paul's injunctions are against "unnatural" behavior. The Kinsey Institute's statistics of the 1950's show that ten percent of Americans are homosexual. That minority of us is part of nature and of its laws, too. Can we claim to love the Creator if we despise the creation? I'm not saying that every homosexual person is without sin. Rape, child molesting, sexual coercion of any kind is sinful. But the fact is that these aberrations are far more prevalent among heterosexual males than among homosexuals of either gender.

I have seen great improvement in the last few years in the attitude towards homosexuals, largely due to the efforts of brave men and women who write, sing, dance, and celebrate their experience for the better understanding of us all. I no longer have to confine my reading to books like the one that made me cry on the airplane. Most bookstores, and certainly all women's bookstores, have dozens of works by lesbian and gay authors who can teach us the positive, joyful, funny aspects of their lives: Rita Mae Brown, Adrienne Rich, Barbara Deming, Sheila Ortiz Taylor, Harvey Fierstein, James Baldwin, and Christopher Isherwood, to mention only a few.

But there is still a long way to go until discrimination in jobs, housing, and child custody, is a thing of the past. There is a long way to go until the parents of homosexual children are free to love them completely without fear or shame. There is a long way to go before gay men and lesbians no longer think it's a big deal when ten parents march the length of Market Street in San Francisco as we did in the Freedom Day Parade.

So while it was a heady experience for Bob and I to be the object of such love and gratitude, I look forward to the day when declaring our love for all our children will not be such a remarkable event.

Magic Yellow Button

by Shirley Powers

I am the author of With No Slow Dance *(Palo Alto, CA: Two Steps In Press, 1980). I have also been published in many small press magazines. I am a musician and composer, single parent, and teach piano lessons for basic survival. When I am not marching in Gay Freedom Day parades, I combine my poetry and compositions into multimedia performances.*

Magic Yellow Button

Wearing that small yellow button
with its political slogan,
I march between police barricades
under thousands of lavender balloons
Rows of cheering, applauding bystanders
crowd ten to twenty deep behind
bicycle racks,
racks that will hold bright colored
back to school bicycles
another morning

So many buttons I have worn
in so many marches,
... U.S. out of Vietnam ... No more Nukes
... Free Huey Newton
receiving jeers, thrown eggs,
my motherly concern growing
over your safety, as I pushed
you along the march route
in your baby stroller
Startled now by the spectators'
cheers on this Gay Freedom Day,
thinking perhaps I should smile
and wave, like a hero in a ticker tape
parade, I walk under the applause drawing
banner, whose words match
my yellow button
    "Parents of Lesbians and Gays"
Parent, for the simple act of
birthing you, who then
grew to make your own choice

Selected Resources

Books for Parents:

Back, Gloria Guss. *Are You Still My Mother? Are You Still My Family?* Warner Books, 1985.

Berrzon, Betty. *Positively Gay.* Mediamix Associates, 1984.

Boggan, E. Carrington, et al. *Rights of Gay People: An ACLU Handbook.* Bantam, 1983.

Borhek, Mary. *Coming Out to Parents.* Pilgrim Press, 1983.

Brown, Howard. *Familiar Faces, Hidden Lives.* Harcourt Brace Jovanovitch, 1979.

Clark, Don. *Loving Someone Gay.* Signet Books, 1978.

Fairchild, Betty and Nancy Hayward. *Now That You Know: What Every Parent Should Know About Homosexuality.* Harcourt Brace Jovanovitch, 1979.

Griffin, Carolyn, and Marilyn and Art Wirth. *Beyond Acceptance.* Prentice Hall, Inc., 1986. *The most recent book for parents — well written and helpful.*

Herron, Ann. *One Teenager in Ten.* Alyson Publications, 1983.

Scanzoni, Letha and Virginia Ramey Mollenkott. *Is the Homosexual My Neighbor?* Harper & Row, 1978.

About Lesbianism:

Adair, Nancy. *Word is Out.* New Glide Publications, 1978. *Also a film — described in Reva Tow's story.*

Beck, Evelyn Torton, ed. *Nice Jewish Girls: A Lesbian Anthology.* Crossing Press, 1982.

Biren, Joan. *Eye to Eye: Portraits of Lesbians.* Glad Hag Books, 1979.

Gomez, Alma, Cherrie Moraga, and Mariana Romo-Carmona. *Cuentos: Stories by Latinas.* Kitchen Table Press, 1983.

Grahn, Judy. *Another Mother Tongue: Gay Words, Gay Worlds.* Beacon Press, 1984. *History and culture of homosexuality.*

Jullion, Jeanne. *Long Way Home: The Odyssey of A Lesbian Mother & Her Children.* Cleis Press, 1985. *The chronicle of a custody case which took place during "the headiest times" of gay political history.*

Martin, Del and Phyllis Lyon. *Lesbian / Woman.* Bantam, 1977.

Moraga, Cherrie and Gloria Anzaldua. *This Bridge Called My Back: Writings by Radical Women of Color.* Kitchen Table Press, 1981.

Smith, Barbara, ed. *Home Girls: A Black Feminist Anthology.* Kitchen Table Press, 1983.

Vida, Ginny, ed. *Our Right to Love: A Lesbian Resource Book.* Prentice-Hall, 1978. *A good reference book.*

Zanetti, Barbara ed. *A Faith of One's Own: Explorations by Catholic Lesbians.* Crossing Press, 1986.

Parents and Friends of Lesbians and Gays:

PFLAG is a non-profit federation active throughout the United States and in other countries. For a contact in your locality write to: PFLAG, P.O. Box 24565, Los Angeles, CA 90024.

A multilingual booklet entitled "About Our Children" is available free of charge from PFLAG. Published in English, Chinese, French, Japanese and Spanish, it's a good introduction to the group's attitudes towards homosexuality as well as an informative comfort for parents new to dealing with the issue. (Send a long self-addressed stamped envelope with your request).

In addition, PFLAG has available other publications and both audio and video cassettes on different aspects of homosexuality, such as biblical and theological backgrounds on homosexuality, gays and lesbians in history and literature, homosexuality in the Black community, and issues of concern to openly gay teachers. There is a specific tape for parents on coming out to family and friends. For a list of audio and video cassettes send a self-addressed stamped envelope to the PFLAG headquarters in Los Angeles. PFLAG can also furnish speakers for organizations and community groups and has a lending library open to both groups and individuals.

About the Editor

Louise Rafkin (b. 1958) is a writer, graphic artist and journalist whose articles and fiction have appeared in many progressive, lesbian and gay, and feminist publications. In 1986 she received the National Gay and Lesbian Press Association's Outstanding Achievement Award in Opinion, Commentary and Column writing for her work in *Coming Up!*, San Francisco's lesbian and gay newspaper.

Currently living in Oakland, California, she is working on several writing projects, including a novel, and is student of Kajukenbo Kung Fu.

Cleis Press is a seven-year-old women's publishing
company committed to publishing progressive
books by women.

If you wish to order from Cleis Press please contact the office nearest
you: Cleis East, PO Box 8933, Pittsburgh PA 15221 or Cleis West, PO
Box 14684, San Francisco CA 94114. Individual orders must be pre-
paid and include 15% shipping. PA and CA residents add sales tax.
MasterCard and Visa orders welcome — include account number, exp.
date, signature and (MasterCard only) 4-digit bank number.

Books from Cleis Press

Sex Work: Writings by Women in the Sex Industry edited by Frederique Delacoste and Priscilla Alexander. ISBN: 0-939416-10-7 24.95 cloth; ISBN: 0-939416-11-5 9.95 paper.

Different Daughters: A Book by Mothers of Lesbians edited by Louise Rafkin. ISBN: 0-939416-12-3 21.95 cloth; ISBN: 0-939416-13-1 8.95 paper.

The Little School: Tales of Disappearance & Survival in Argentina by Alicia Partnoy. ISBN: 0-939416-08-5 15.95 cloth; ISBN: 0-939416-07-7 8.95 paper.

With the Power of Each Breath: A Disabled Women's Anthology edited by Susan Browne, Debra Connors & Nanci Stern. ISBN: 0- 939416-09-3 24.95 cloth; ISBN: 0-939416-06-9 9.95 paper.

Long Way Home: The Odyssey of a Lesbian Mother & Her Children by Jeanne Jullion. ISBN: 0-939416-05-0 8.95 paper.

The Absence of the Dead Is Their Way of Appearing by Mary Winfrey Trautmann. ISBN: 0-939416-04-2 8.95 paper.

Woman-Centered Pregnancy & Birth by the Federation of Feminist Women's Health Centers. ISBN: 0-939416-03-4 11.95 paper.

Voices in the Night: Women Speaking About Incest edited by Toni A.H. McNaron & Yarrow Morgan. ISBN: 0-939416-02-6 8.95 paper.

Fight Back! Feminist Resistance to Male Violence edited by Frederique Delacoste & Felice Newman. ISBN: 0-939416-01-8 13.95 paper.

On Women Artists: Poems 1975-1980 by Alexandra Grilikhes. ISBN: 0-939416-00-X 4.95 paper.